Cast aside morals, don't stick to the law,
Let us follow perversions openly, spontaneously.

...

Nothing is sacred. The whole universe
should be the prey of our ferocious demands.
Commit your rogueries often, in manifold ways,
Let Sin gain power in your soul.
Repeat your attempts in cynicism,
Let each new step lead to greater crimes.
After many a lovely year, jeering at God,
We shall return to the bosom of Nature,
Where it will not matter whether we shall gain
Reward or death — its crucible will swallow you and spit you out.
For everything will reappear again in nature,
Servant and master, spouse or whore,
Because Nature loves us equally,
Whether we are chaste or scoundrelly.

    Marquis de Sade, 'The Truth'

'I find it particularly dangerous if someone is virtuous in
a depraved age. Such an eccentricity makes happiness impossible — virtue leads into isolation. It is much wiser to
be a sinner like everybody else, than to be honest, standing
alone.'

    Marquis de Sade, 'Juliette'

'No part of this story is true. Just the whole of it.'

    János Kenedi

Do It Yourself
Hungary's Hidden Economy

János Kenedi

Pluto Press

First English edition published by Pluto Press Limited,
Unit 10 Spencer Court, 7 Chalcot Road, London NW1 8LH

Copyright © János Kenedi

ISBN 0 86104 344 8

Cover drawing by Chris Madden
Cover design by Clive Challis

Typeset by Grassroots Typeset, London NW6 6PS
Printed in Great Britain by Photobooks (Bristol) Limited,
28 Midland Road, St Philips, Bristol.

Contents

Introduction:
Opposition in Hungary Today

It is often suggested that Hungary has no movement of opposition, unlike Poland with KOR and Solidarity, or Czechoslovakia with Charter 77. The implication is that the Kadar regime has provided its citizens with better living standards and greater cultural and political freedoms than exist in any other East European country; and that it has attained a popular legitimacy that prevents the emergence of any dissent.

So, it came as a surprise to Western observers, and possibly to the Hungarian authorities too, when in October 1979 some 250 Hungarian intellectuals signed letters of protest against the sentences delivered in the Prague trials of Charter 77 activists. This was not their first act in support of their Czech comrades, for already in January 1977 some 34 Hungarians had publicly expressed their support for the Charter. Indeed it was under the influence of Charter 77 that a new wave of dissident, samizdat (unofficial publishing) activity developed in Hungary at the end of the 1970s, stressing the issue of human rights. Many of the initiators of the movement were veterans of earlier struggles. The first significant one of these to emerge since the 1956 revolution was the Vietnam Solidarity Commission in the mid-sixties. Its leaders included several maoist-inclined students who criticised the Hungarian regime for abandoning socialist and marxist principles. The Czechoslovak reform movement of 1968 then led to the emergence of more reformist dissidents who defended the Dubcek experiment and favoured similar economic and political reforms in Hungary.

The arrest and trial in 1973 of the former maoist Miklós Haraszti for distributing copies of his book on life in a Budapest factory (*A Worker in a Workers' State*, Penguin 1978) brought these previously separate groups together to demand an end to censorship. That year an important campaign began around the personal problems of everyday life in Hungary — over 1500 signatures were collected for a petition against a new law that sought to restrict the right to abortion. This campaign drew into the movement many members of a younger generation less concerned with ideological questions who were to become the backbone of a number of samizdat organisations that emerged in 1977. They constituted the free university seminars that arose on the model of the earlier Czech and Polish flying universities.

Today, the Hungarian samizdat has its own 'bookshop' and its own catalogue of publications. Its activists have rejected clandestine ways of organising and work openly in an attempt to exercise the rights that, according to the letter of the constitution, they enjoy. Besides the translation of a number of western books, and of articles by Hungarian writers published only in the West, the samizdat has produced three major volumes of writings by Hungarian dissidents. *Marxism in the Fourth Decade*, a collection of current assessments of marxism and its relevance for Eastern Europe, appeared at the end of 1977. *Profile*, edited by János Kenedi and published in 1978, comprised 34 articles all previously refused publication in official journals. More recently, following the death in 1979 of István Bibó, the influential political theorist and government minister during the 1956 revolution, a thousand-page memorial volume has been circulated. The samizdat has produced reports on the repression of religious minorities like the Methodists, on the imprisonment of workers and peasants for political 'crimes', and on the problems of underprivileged groups like newly urbanised workers and gypsies. In 1980, SZETA, the Fund to Support the Poor, was set up to draw attention to the plight of Hungary's poor and to raise funds through concerts and art exhibitions. When Polish workers went on strike in Gdanzk in August 1980, seven Hungarians planned to fly there to express their support and solidarity. All seven — amongst them János Kenedi — were prevented from leaving Budapest airport and had their passports confiscated.

The Hungarian opposition has not yet attained the same social or political significance as the Czech Chartists or the Polish KOR but they have over the past years broadened their scope to take in the personal and social problems of everyday life. In this process, János Kenedi has played a key role. Almost unique amongst the dissidents of his generation for not having emerged from a marxist background, his primary concern has always been for the existential problems of real life, and his activities represent an attempt to live a free, decent and human existence in a society that claims such a life as its ideal but systematically denies and represses it in practice.

Bill Lomax
Nottingham, May 1981.

Bill Lomax is the author of *Hungary 1956*, Allison & Busby 1976, editor of *Eyewitness in Hungary*, Spokesman 1980.

'Private Sector'

In the Hungarian political economy all enterprises are, in theory, state-owned. However, to compensate for the built-in inflexibilities of large organisations — especially in the services sector — individual craft workers and artisans are allowed to operate under certain conditions. They are fully licensed by local authorities, but heavily taxed and not permitted to employ more than a few helpers — 'exploitation of labour' having been abolished, and no scope allowed for 'budding capitalists'. This in turn, has given rise to contractors, go-betweens, people who oil the contacts between state firms, individual operators and final customers. This is the 'private sector', in contrast to the 'state sector'.

1. Buying the Property

In 1969, my mother acquired a bedsit-type flat in a new housing development through her backdoor contacts for next to nothing — about 20-odd thousand forints. I didn't appreciate its value at the time. I lived there with my first wife and our child for about six months, then decided to move back to my mother's bungalow in the green belt. We hadn't felt at home on the raw new estate; besides, my son is asthmatic, and doctors were advising us to move to a more rural area.

I was ashamed of my mother's manipulations and wouldn't countenance the idea of making a profit. I asked for an estimate from a private-sector builder, for work I'd need done on our green-belt residence. He quoted 80,000 forints. My neighbour on the estate jumped at the chance of acquiring the flat next door to him and paid the money without batting an eyelid. He would break down the dividing wall between the two flats to make a three-room flat, he said — what's the use of dividing walls when you could hear even the slightest cough through them, anyway? I was indifferent to his plans. A flat is a flat is a flat.

To my somewhat didactic way of thinking, the equation meant: flat acquired by fiddling + moral reluctance + enough money for new flat = new flat + moral well-being. The negative factor of moral reluctance was offset by the positive factor of moral well-being. I was a student at the time. This kind of moralising provided a natural antidote to the aridity of my studies. Maintaining my personal integrity was an attempt to create a bridge between economic laws and public morals. So refusing to make a profit from wheeler-dealing in property became morally uplifting. With that equation, and its moral content, I felt I had established the correct relationship with the world; I could rightly belong to that one-sixth part of it where higher social values are the governing ones. I was duly proud of my moral superiority.

When it came to signing the contract, my neighbour arrived with two strangers. Apparently overcome by his beneficence, he stammered he'd decided to hand over my old flat to his homeless friends. It would be unseemly for him to expand while others had no roof over their head.

I was quite touched by this act of brotherly goodwill; at least my unearned advantage would benefit someone in need. This glow of moral satisfaction lasted until I started talking to the newcomers. It turned out that my good neighbour had passed my flat to them for 220,000 forints. My moral stance had cost me 140,000 forints. My neighbour pocketed the difference before my very eyes. I doubt whether I learned as much in my five years at university as I did in those five minutes. All the knowledge acquired at the fountainhead of learning never yielded that much money.

But not even this lesson shook my faith in mathematically expressed moral principles. I had opted for theoretical subjects in my studies. My chief interest lay in a conceptual approach to fundamental reality. This affront to my moral standards would, I felt, merely enhance the purity of theoretical thought.

I was a member of a discussion group on problems of social theory. My colleagues and I had thrown away our lecture notes and embarked on reading the socialist classics. Our aim was to distil the brew until only pure essence remained. The solvent we used was pure mathematics and higher economics. Thus we hoped to find the ultimate model of true socialism. We were confident we would find it in time. We had shown persistence and scientific ambition at university. In our final year, we envisaged a future as a scientific team, continuing our work in an institute of social planning. Unfortunately, there wasn't anybody prepared to employ us as a team. Well, if we couldn't work together, we could still spend all our free time together. We would form a commune and live together, until we could persuade some institute to take us all on.

I got a job at a research institute, as a scientific trainee. The only thing I wasn't allowed to touch was my chief interest: my contribution to building the ultimate joint global theory. So, when my job came up for renewal, I took no steps to keep it. I opted to become a freelance translator.

Some members of our discussion group started to climb the establishment ladder, in the hope that from the top they would be better able to aid the purpose of the team. Others didn't bother to start the climb and forgot about the team. Others turned their backs on both the ladder and team and went out into the wide world to find the 'weakest link'. Or something else. I was left alone, with grand ideas far beyond the scientific capabilities of one person, and a programme of collective living.

About six years after the morally fortifying sale of the reprehensibly acquired flat, I began to have doubts about the validity of the equation so confidently formulated at university. I was then living with my second wife in my father's flat, but a deadline was hanging over us. It was the last year of my father's contract as a surgeon in Nigeria. We had to find somewhere to live, sooner rather than later. I had left the divided half of my mother's flat to my first wife and my son. We had no savings whatsoever. My only property was a Zhiguli car — alas, not even a Dormobile. Its value in 1975 was exactly the same as the price I'd got for the flat in 1969. But for 80,000 forints I wouldn't have been able to buy a rathole.

Against the depreciation of money and the growth in demand for housing, only one thing remained stable: the value of string-pulling. I discovered a hidden error in my equation, once mathematics had been modified by the rules of real life: a flat acquired by pulling strings is *not equal* to any other flat.

The decisive error was not the sale of the flat without making a profit (that is, my mistake in mixing morality with economics). My assumption that one flat could be exchanged for another wasn't a cardinal error either. My unforgiveable sin had been to exchange the proceeds of string-pulling for money and thus to disregard the advantages of the 'planned' economy over those of the market.

Of course, if I hadn't thrown away my notes, I could have learnt that what they taught at university was true — only real life is somewhat different. I might have avoided my fundamental error if I'd known about the secondary planned economy, in which scarce goods are distributed by personal allocation. I stumbled on this truth only after squandering my share of the spoils. Having blown my inheritance, I had to stand on my own two feet.

We had to find somewhere to live, somehow. Without money, influence, or a place on the housing list, there was great scope for daydreaming. Our first idea was a commune. We asked around our friends. Could our collective meagre resources add up to the price of a house? We looked at the prices of 4-5 room

houses or flats and dropped the idea. Next we thought of a peasant cottage on the outskirts of the city. But the intelligentsia
had started moving into the villages, only to meet there the
agricultural workers streaming into industry from farther out,
so the prices of acceptable peasant cottages had also rocketed.

We hadn't even started, and already were stumbling onto
dangerous ground. We were stepping out on the road reserved
for people of modest means. Not only was it overcrowded, but
we would have to compete with others of less modest means.
Having no means whatsoever, we could only be losers.

So it seemed we would have to disregard all earth-bound
calculations. Why worry about cash, when we hadn't got any?
So we opted instead for higher social planning. Once a goal is
set, people create suitable conditions for its achievement. That's
how socialism is built. Accordingly, we declared our aims and
left the possibilities to catch up with us later. Our example would
be the state which pursues a deliberate policy of indebtedness.
Henceforth brains would rule, not money.

With the help of a journalist friend — one who opposed in
the strongest possible terms our ideas about communes and
peasant cottages — we placed a deliberately vague small ad in a
paper. The ad immediately opened up aspects of reality not visible from the depths of our financial status. Out of 300 replies,
two nearly led to something.

The first was an offer of a two-storey house, with two flats,
in a residential area, in the hilly outskirts of the city. It had been
built by a private sector builder on spec. The work was of quite
high quality. He asked 1,400,000 forints. Of course, we didn't
have the cash, but there was an asset which indicated our
seriousness: a friend who had a flat nearer the centre was willing
to come in with us. That would have taken care of half the asking price.

Next, my father came home for a short visit from Africa.
He took a look at the housing situation and, suitably horrified,
told us we could do what we liked with his flat — we could even
sell it, provided we reserved a room for him when he finally
returned. With this, he briskly flew back to the Third World.

This could have covered the rest of the price. And the sale
of my car, a building society loan, a small sum promised by my
mother and every conceivable personal loan would have enabled

us to build an extra one-room flat for my father on the roof. Alas, my friend cried off at the last minute. The attractions of the city centre proved too strong for him.

The second opportunity — at 1,200,000 forints — turned out to be a ramshackle old building, in the middle of a huge overgrown garden. The seller took it for granted that we wouldn't bother about the state of the house itself. It was ready for demolition, and we could knock at least 200,000 off the price to cover the cost of demolishing it. But we didn't want to build a brand new palace in the manorial grounds; all we wanted was two flats. This was not so much a question of engineering, considering the state of the old house, but of whether we could afford it.

Unfortunately, negotiations ran into personal difficulties. The owner, a fire brigade chief, took fright, partly because he thought his sudden gain might prove embarrassing, partly because of his character. Both scruples could be traced back to his high rank as a public official, which made it possible for him to get a luxury council flat out of turn, despite the fact that he already had a more modest one. He had intended to pass on the old flat to his elderly parents, who were living in the derelict house — but now he became afraid that an underhand reshuffle might compromise him.

His own advertisement had been pretty vague to begin with, and so was his reply to ours. He too had been hoping to pick up tips from replies to his ad. The difference between us was that we were determined to spend our imaginary million forints as soon as we'd viewed the noble ruin in the middle of a jungle, while he remained doubtful about the whole project. He insisted on telephone conversations under false names (we were never allowed to call him), on semi-secret meetings in coffee-houses, where he was suspicious even of the regulars, mostly elderly ladies. Together we went on Sunday excursions to the hills; we sat in secluded forest clearings, scratching in the dust with a twig the complex moves from flat to flat and house to house. He dropped envelopes in our letterbox (addressed in letters elaborately cut out from newspapers) containing railway tickets for a return trip to Debrecen, so that we could negotiate in secret on the train. I had to watch the most boring football match of the season to discuss with him the methodology of transferring funds.

The negotiations neared completion. We agreed that my friend would act as a stooge in the chief's second flat for a while, taking down the rubbish so that the janitor got used to him.

The nearer we got to closing the deal, the more paranoid he became. On one occasion, we had agreed to meet secretly at a street-corner somewhere in the suburds, but he just passed us by, indicating with a wink that he was being followed. We didn't share his persecution complex and were really keen on the property, but the more we fell in with his tortuous safety measures, the more elusive he became. In the end, when we were on a good way towards solving our housing problem by becoming candidates for the lunatic asylum, he dropped us.

Meanwhile, we spotted another small ad that did not require a codebreaker. This concerned a 1,000 square yard plot with a half-built house on a hill in the outskirts, for 700,000 forints. This really was a very good proposition. In the case of the first deal, we would have had to pay the actual building costs twice — the builder understandably wanted to double the value of his property — at 1,500 forints per square yard — by adding to it the value of his labour and materials. The second deal would have meant taking part in the risks of a complicated reshuffle involving the various council flats plus our own dwellings, not to mention the fact that it would all have been delayed for at least a year, what with phoney registrations of phoney owners, selling our own flats, official approval of a host of contracts, and so on. Only then would we have been able to start rebuilding; and the cost of materials was steadily increasing.

In this latest offer, they were charging only 200,000 forints for the building work, over and above the price of the plot. The area of the plot — and its cost, at 300 forints per square yard — was only one third the cost of the fire chief's property. Admittedly, the whole neighbourhood was a wilderness. The only snag was that the 700,000 forints were now unavailable. My journalist friend — once bitten by the fire chief — dropped out of the consortium.

So I was going to have to look for a proper business partner, preferably someone who had some idea about building operations. I couldn't expect anything from my high-minded literary friends. But at various noisy parties I occasionally met an engineer who was conspicuous by his silence and who I therefore felt must know something the others didn't. I accosted him at the next opportunity. He answered my roundabout queries with some quite practical counter-questions. So disregarding the currently fashionable denigration of ruling cadres, I applied the standard techniques of personal cadre-selection.

It turned out that he would have scored highly in an earlier period, when a worker/peasant origin carried a bonus. However, since the peasantry had moved into industry and the workers increasingly busied themselves with horticulture, (thereby messing up the class distinctions laid down in text-books) his origins didn't represent such a great asset. The declining prestige of his parents also meant they were now less favoured with earthly goods. His father had seen no future for his son at the collective farm, and sent him off to the technical university. He struggled through college and married a fellow-student. His in-laws, engaged in the more profitable export trade, endowed his wife with a dowry: a tiny house on a 30-square yard plot, on a barren hillside on the outskirts of the town. That gave him barely enough room for his morning press-ups; he was interested in my plan, so we formed a partnership without any further ado. The sale of their little house ensured that the first instalments payable for the new property would be available. We took the first step towards a two-flat dwelling to be built by our own efforts in partnership.

Once we showed that we were in earnest, we succeeded by judicious haggling in beating down the original price by 60,000 forints — thanks to my friend's engineering knowledge. He worked out that the value of the unfinished building had been put at 100,000 above the going rate. Of course, the owners could have found someone else, more likely to fork out 700,000 forints but they were coming dangerously close to divorce court proceedings, and therefore to dividing the spoils of marriage. The property was in the wife's name as her parents had bought the plot and — according to her — paid for the building operations. These were executed by the husband, who, understandably, wanted to establish before the court that the cost of the building work had come out of his own pocket. If he had stuck stubbornly to the 700,000 forints price, he could have come off badly. Without a sale before judgement, there was a danger that the whole property, plot, house and all, might go to the wife.

To shorten the delay, and cover at least the value of his labour, he agreed to the drop in price. The wife — rightly or wrongly — felt she had been short-changed by 60,000. We had gained that much but we had also caused a crisis. The couple stopped talking to one another, heralding untold danger for us. By basing our partnership on the breakup of another we didn't know what we were letting ourselves in for.

Once my partner's cottage was sold we had half the buying price in hand. But we didn't get much nearer to restarting the building operations — the money was needed for the first steps towards signing the contract. Luckily the state helps would-be house-owners with lots of things, including a generous helping of bureaucracy. Where would we be if, between seller and buyer there weren't the council housing department, the excise, the land registry? Just handing over 640,000 and being done with it might lead to rampant profiteering, and worse!

The state knows the cares and worries of house-buyers well and helps in drawing up the terms of payment. When contracts are exchanged you only have to put down about half the price of the property. The other half is advanced by the state — at a stiff interest rate — 17 per cent of the official property valuation. This, of course, is a mere formality, not to be confused with the facts.

It is the common interest of sellers and buyers that the state should grab 17 per cent of as small a sum as possible. The state may be the universal builder, it may benevolently give us credit, but it was not building either our house or that of the divorced couple. We were ready to do homage to the state, but we jibbed at the 17 per cent.

The regulations couldn't be changed, but the basic sum could. Our solicitor prepared a contract showing a 350,000 forints sale price; then we had to swear — without witnesses — that we hadn't seen him making out another contract quoting 640,000 forints. This second contract was deposited with a public notary. Once the first, fictitious contract was stamped and approved by the council housing department, the real contract would enter into force. I paid 350,000 forints to the solicitor on one side of the notary's desk; he handed over the same sum to the owner standing at the other side of the desk.

The guarantee to the owner that we would eventually pay her the remaining 290,000 forints was the knowledge that if we refused, she could disclose the stamp duty fiddle, declare the fictitious contract to be the ruling one and prove that the legal contract was fictitious. We had no second thoughts about paying up — but first the fictitious contract had to be officially approved.

Turning a fictitious contract into a legal one is a simple matter, compared with the contortions on the financial side. Admittedly, it is not too difficult while the financial wrangling is going on between the seller and buyer, the third party being there only in spirit — although it is because of this third party that the dual contract is necessary. Final approval, however, is possible only when the spirit is incarnated in the person of a salaried employee of the state: the valuer. The state could dispense with valuers by setting up a complete land register. One could then simply look up the price of such and such a property. However, instead of such a gigantic ledger, the council employs official valuers, who have all the data in their heads.

A valuer can follow the book or he can behave like a human being. A valuer following the book is hopeless. If he behaves like a human being he will use his head — meaning he will accept a bribe.

The question is: how much? Official approval was worth 49,300 forints to us — the difference between 17 per cent of 640,000 and 17 per cent of 350,000. If the valuer followed the book (and had some inkling of the hidden contract) he would claim 108,000 forints for the state. If he behaved like a human being, he might want part of the difference. There is nothing to prevent him declaring that the property is worth 700,000 forints, or even more; but he probably wouldn't want to cause the deal to flounder by overvaluing. As a human being, he will try to find a golden mean.

The snag is that one cannot put a value on the valuer's golden mean. For this, we would need unofficial valuers valuing the official valuers' values. Luckily, there are some well-established customs. According to our solicitor, valuers usually claimed 1 per cent of the purchase price stated in the contract — but the minimum of 5,000 forints for their highly responsible work. 5,000 forints was worth 49,300 to us; to the valuer it was worth 5,000 not to push up the value of the property to the figure at which he might suspect it would eventually change hands.

Following this lecture on the tribal customs of valuers, our solicitor gave us the name of the only valuer on the council notorious for not accepting bribes. Luckily, the person designated to deal with me was not this exceptional character. With a light heart, I drove to the council offices, to pick up the valuer and take him to the property.

Valuation doesn't seem to be a very time-consuming task. After a few minutes' survey, we were back in the car. Valuation of the envelope I handed over took even less time: a glance at the thickness of the envelope and the colour of the banknote shining through its transparent window convinced the valuer that the property was not worth more than 350,000 forints.

This was the first bribe I gave in respect of the building operations, but the technique wasn't new to me. For the past five years, whenever I bought a car at the official price, the envelope made sure of the correct number of spare parts, otherwise unobtainable in the market.

The final reckoning threw up interesting figures. $640,000 - 350,000 = 49,300$ for us, less 5,000; $X - 350,000 = 5,000$ to the valuer; $X - 350,000 = 59,500$ to the state. Not quite in accordance with the laws of mathematics as taught at university.

The fictitious contract thus became officially approved. However, unexpected complications arose about the payment of the hidden balance. Not that we did not scrape the money together: I sold my car for 80,000 forints, my mother unexpectedly coughed up 75,000 (perhaps in recognition of my honesty over the sale of her council flat); 200,000 forints were borrowed from a friend of my wife, at 5 per cent interest per annum. The friend's father, a private sector button manufacturer, kept a large number of savings books with his daughter. We borrowed four books, at 50,000 forints each, and promised the woman to return them within a few weeks in case the father looked for them — which was unlikely anyway. By that time we should have received our loan from the state building society. So we were keen to pay off the remaining 290,000 forints to begin the building work. A date was fixed with the woman — the nominal owner — for handing over the money; then the husband pulled the rug from under our feet.

Two days before the appointed date the solicitor phoned to

tell me the deal was off, we would have to save what we could from the ruins. It turned out that our solicitor had received a letter from the husband's solicitor. The husband had got to know we had signed a contract of sale with his wife concerning the property, without his consent, despite it being listed as joint property in the submission to the divorce court. As the building work had been started during the marriage, anything on the plot was deemed to be a joint acquisition. And the husband's solicitor petitioned the court to charge the outcome of the financial settlement against the value of the property — to which the court acceded.

This meant that our contract with the wife became null and void, as it explicitly specified that the property was unencumbered; now it had became encumbered, subject to court proceedings. Our solicitor pointed out that our position was disastrous: we had handed over 350,000 forints to the wife which could not be claimed back, as it was paid out against a valid contract. All we could do was wait for the decision on sharing out of goods and chattels. This might take years, during which time, of course, no building could take place. Furthermore, the building society was only allowed to lend on the security of unencumbered property. This meant there was nothing from which to pay back the personal loans.

The husband's action was wicked but understandable. He had taken part in our discussions quite frequently before the contract was signed, but when he accepted the reduction of 60,000 forints, the wife stopped speaking to him and excluded him from all negotiations. We didn't bother to invite him to the exchange of either contract — as the property was in the wife's name and the registry is only interested in the signature of the nominal owner. The husband's move conjured up the threat of another scandalous divorce in my mind's eye: that of myself and my partner. He had sold his cottage with vacant possession by the end of a year, by which time our new house should have been completed. I could perhaps have put the three of them up for a few months; but dreaded what my father would say to enforced communality. He was due back within the year.

Our solicitor devised a devastatingly simple measure of desperation. The plan relied for its effect on the workings of bureaucracy. He took the unstamped third copy of the fictitious

— but legally valid — contract (kept for information only, otherwise not worth the paper it was written on) put it in an envelope and posted it by express mail to the land registry. He reckoned it would arrive sooner than the notification from the divorce court, and get registered with a lower reference number than the court document. It didn't matter that the first one was worthless, the second valid. The court's letter could not be opened before the document with the lower number was dealt with. The official at the registry would obviously notice that the document was incomplete, indeed worthless. However, instead of tossing it into his waste-paper basket — what's the use of an agreement between two private persons without the signature and stamp of the official valuer? — he would dictate a reply to the sender, requesting the negligent solicitor to submit the correct document within 30 days. If 30 days were not enough to twist the arm of the recalcitrant husband, our solicitor would draw out the time further with additional faulty documents. This might damage his reputation within the profession but it would improve it among his clients.

The plan depended on the administration's slothfulness on the one hand, its commitment to unshakeably correct procedure on the other. Our faith wasn't misplaced. Officialdom does not play fast and loose with the client. The land registry conscientiously sent one request after another to the solicitor. With our back thus covered by the forces of bureaucracy, we confronted the couple directly. We told them we had a valid contract clearly stating that the property was unencumbered; we had nothing to do with their divorce suit. However, we didn't put all our trust in the moral force of our arguments. We told the husband that, according to our two contracts, the maximum he could demand from his wife before the court was the 290,000 forints as yet unpaid against the hidden contract. We would be prepared to deposit this sum with a solicitor, provided he withdrew his application to the court; subject to the court's decision, he could then collect his share from this sum.

The wife was then given a guarantee that she would receive the remainder of this sum; but she had to accept the settlement. Otherwise we wouldn't pay out the 290,000 forints — after all, the state had valued the property as worth only 350,000 forints, while she had had the gall to ask 640,000 for it. She would have to pay her husband whatever share he was awarded from the 350,000 forints she'd already pocketed from us.

And what if the woman waved the hidden contract at the court hearing? Well, that would only prove that we in our innocence had been prepared to pay an extortionate price — luckily for us the conscientious valuer defended the interests of honest citizens!

Our ultimatum was accepted by both parties. Thus, depositing the 290,000 forints, we ensured that the value of the erstwhile joint property would be shared out justly, according to the rightful judgement of the independent judiciary.

The plot on the hill was ours. It was December and we could start arranging for the various building permits. It was fairly easy to wipe the name of the previous builder off the board at the foot of the plot, but, alas, we couldn't maintain the momentum.

It's just not that simple. Think of it: one could pick up a few bricks, put one on top of the other, and hey presto! a house. What an idea! Everybody would walk around with bricks under their arms, putting up walls any old way, as the spirit moved them. What would the city look like? You'd get round, hexagonal and rhomboid houses.

Amazing, the ideas some people have! One never knows what they might fancy — that's why we have to have rules, for planning, zoning, roofing, facing. Otherwise, the whole town would look like a huge gypsy camp.

Prevention is better than punishment. That's why there are various official bodies entrusted with upholding the building regulations and issuing permits. They also stand there, all helpfulness, between the plot and the finished house — just like the institutions regulating property rights that come between seller and buyer.

There are two official bodies, one charged with the supervision of external beauty, the other with that of internal utility. They are both highly responsible organs, imbued with the principles of harmony and balance. A committee, set up by the city council, ensures that proposed buildings would fit into the cityscape. To safeguard local regulations, the plan also has to go to the building department of the borough council. The members of the first body are public-spirited architects. In the second, authority is represented by council experts. You have to observe the correct order. Only after the committee has approved the externals can one present the plans to the borough council. But there is no rigid, blinkered attitude in the decision-making. The borough council can approve a plan rejected by the committee, or disallow one favoured by it. Furthermore, both of them have the right to accept or reject external as well as internal features. There is no favouritism, nobody can complain, equality reigns. As a result, there are lots of nice, boring houses being built.

We had modified the previous owner's building plan, so we had to put ours on the assembly line, through city council to borough council. It was approved by the first; and rejected by the second. A short note to this effect also summoned us to appear before the borough architect. No explanation was given.

I went round the neighbourhood to find out what was what. The unanimous opinion of all householders in the area was that the architect would be upset by the offer of a bribe. This was a piece of spine-chilling news; the rest was relatively reassuring. The same architect had rejected the plans of every single house-builder. There were a few who failed even at the first hurdle — yet in the end their houses did grow out of the ground. On the other hand, there must have been quite a few people discouraged by these refusals: there were plenty of vacant plots.

In my nightmares, I visualised this ghoul of the hillside as an impeccably dressed, clean-shaven, well-brushed petty official, someone who rigidly stuck to the soulless precepts of the building regulations. To my surprise, I encountered instead a young man of my own age, clad in jeans, long-haired and bearded, much like myself. He listed the enclosures missing from our submission in the friendliest manner; in their absence, he hadn't even opened our file.

It took two months to collect the necessary documents, from five different authorities, including the chimney sweep. A few weeks after I presented them, he summoned me again, to give me another rejection.

His beard had grown longer in the meantime, his manner was even friendlier, as he told me he had to reject the plan. Strictly speaking, by artificially dividing the documentation, he could approve my partner's flat, nothing wrong with that. However, far be it from him to create dissent between partners. Alas, the plan for my flat was completely against the rules.

Personally, he said, he rather liked our idea of an open-plan dining room-kitchen; unfortunately, building regulations did not allow them.

"Why?" I asked, immediately realising my question was meaningless. I knew it would be useless to pass the plan back to my own architect: he didn't know anything I didn't about official regulations. And I couldn't be sure a modified plan would get me anything other than another two months' delay.

How could I get round this character? Bribery was out of the question. He wasn't the pen-pusher type either, with whom one could argue. Apparently we both liked the only thing standing between us: the missing wall. We smiled at one another. We scratched our beards in unison.

The question 'Why?' is usually answered in official circles not by giving a reason, but with the words: 'It is against regulations.' That's why it's useless to ask it in the first place. His answer conformed to this custom. However, shaking off my confusion, I was bold enough to add: 'Which?' Whereupon he reached for the rule-book. When he turned back to face me, I spied a shadow of doubt passing his brow. He could not find the appropriate paragraph. This was encouraging. Perhaps he would be forced to give the reason for his refusal.

"In this country, it is the rule that every room must be surrounded by four walls," he said.

"I'm quite prepared to build four walls," I replied, "I'm no traitor to my country."

"Yes, but that means twice four," he smiled. "Nine, in all."

This wasn't my first lesson in new arithmetic since I started the whole business. I knew what he was going to say: "A room and a kitchen are two separate spaces."

I bowed my head. There was this indestructible wall between us and, as there was no regulation stating that it needn't be there, we couldn't demolish it.

I'll be damned if I put up this wall, I thought. What about turning the new mathematics round?

"Nine minus one would still leave four plus four," I ventured, "just about enough for two dwelling spaces, if that's what the country demands."

He shook his head: my maths was still not up to standard.

"Not so," he said. "Nine minus one only leaves four, you see, and that would enclose only one space. And the same space cannot enclose both kitchen and dining room."

"Why?" I asked again, with incredible daring.

"Because the room would stink of cabbage!" came the devastating reply.

Ah, at least we had left the exalted regions of mathematics and were down to earth again. In gastronomy, I felt, I had an even chance against him. "But I'll be the one living with it," I hazarded.

"You're missing the point," he replied. "What if you happen to kick the bucket? What if you sell the house and leave the smell to your successors?"

Foiled again. His expertise in the proprietorial rights of cabbage smell far exceeded mine. I tried to appeal to authority: the council committee had not wrinkled its collective nose, I ventured. That was irrelevant, he said.

I tried to appeal to what I thought we might have in common.

"Listen, not only are the international architectural journals promoting the idea of great open-plan living spaces, the Hungarian ones are too!"

"True... but that presupposes a new architectural culture," came the revealing reply.

So that was it: he was the standard-bearer of higher aesthetics, while I represented the barbarism of cabbage smell. It was I who had been behaving like a petty official, defending my obscurantism. In truth, his line of thinking was the same as mine: gazing at the desirable, not the available.

"Well... what would happen if I pencilled in a line between kitchen and dining room?" I said, offering to cut the Gordian knot.

"Then I would approve the plan," he replied, rising above petty officialdom. He appended his signature to the plan.

2. Income and Expenditure

So there we were with the building-plot, a half-built house on it and not a penny to carry on. We had exchanged all our liquid funds for the property.

The arcitect's estimate for a 100 sq. yd. flat area came to 500,000 forints. After the payment against the phoney contract, I was left with 3,000 forints — just enough to pay the architect for the plans.

My father's town flat was a reserve: it could have been sold for 300,000 forints — provided we disregarded that it was supposed to be collateral of last resort for the loan to be given by the state building society.

Once the seller repaid his loan to the society, we were entitled to apply immediately for the same loan. We did not trust the vexatious litigants to send the money. We sent it ourselves. Once the property was free of mortgage I wrote to the society, asking for an identical loan.

The society sent us a booklet containing the rules and conditions of its credit policy. 'The Hungarian Socialist Workers' (i.e. Communist) Party and the Government are continually making great efforts to improve the housing situation. Their aim is to ensure that every family has a home of its own. The realisation of this aim is a difficult and complicated task. It is well known that, at the time of the Liberation, we inherited not only obsolete political and economic conditions, but also an extremely unfavourable housing situation. Shanty towns, jerrybuilt homes, appalling miners' settlements, millions of mud-walled hovels built without proper foundations, cave-dwellings, communal barracks of estate labourers are almost all things of the past.

I found it curious that a building society should invite applicants for money to a consciousness-raising session. But, bit by bit, I chewed my way through the text. 'The upper limits of the various forms of loans available for house building or purchase are always defined by the ruling credit policies of the state.' But no actual sum was mentioned. The text suggested only 'A sum defined by the principles ruling at the time of approval.' I consulted an official at the SBS as to what this sum might be.

"I take it, my dear sir, that you would like to build a house?" The official leaned back in his chair and crossed his legs. He opened the band holding my personal file together and spread out on the table the architect's estimate. The booklet said: "The basis of credit approval is the building estimate." With his pencil, he pinpointed the words: 'basis of credit'.

"You can't build a house for this little. This estimate is exact to the last penny, as far as current building costs are concerned. But while you are building, the state won't be idle. Prices of building materials are going up all the time."

He pulled an Internal Bulletin from his desk drawer, marked 'Strictly Confidential', and put it in front of me.

"By the time the contract is completed, the price of steel and other materials will have gone up by at least 30 per cent. You don't allow for this in your estimate. The society will only release half the basis of credit — this would be 250,000 forints, if we disregarded the shortcomings of your estimate as we intend to do. The client is important to us and, we hope, the society is equally important to the client. But you must understand we can only release half the sum to begin with, that is, 120,000 forints. It so happens this is the upper limit for family houses. This is the meaning of 'Principles ruling at the time'.

"You will have to establish a credit of 120,000 in favour of the society; then we pay you the sum you loaned to us; then, over 30 years, you repay us in instalments. Is that clear?

"Furthermore, you cannot receive 120,000 forints in a lump sum. You will have to build one tenth of the house from your own funds — only then can we release one tenth of 120,000. Once you reach the stage of one fifth, we give you one fifth of the money. Thus, the money you lent us will be paid out to you according to levels of completion. In other words, the 'basis of credit' is your security.

"What we are offering is Trust. We believe you have the financial means of the building. In exchange for Trust, we only ask for Reliability. You will have to manage from your own funds; we are trusting that you have the necessary money, we shall accept your word, upon which the various tenths will be released. We shall not scrutinise the levels of completion with a fine-toothed comb. We shall believe you when you let us know you're a quarter the way through and release the appropriate percentage.

"We won't ask for bills. Artisans are busy people. If you spent your time looking for those willing to issue invoices your house would never be ready. And the society would suffer if you delayed the repayments. As I said, while you are building, the state won't be idle either. Money is losing its value all the time. However, the society takes the long-term view. To enable us to allow credit to your grandchildren, we shall need your repayments — the sooner the better. We don't want your grandson to inherit your depreciating money — he will have his own worries.

"When you finish building, we shall come out and see whether there is a house at all, whether you succeeded in scraping the money together. If you abuse our trust, we shall auction off your property. That is our ultimate security, as laid down in the contract."

When the contract is signed with the society, security has to be proven, preferably in the form of savings books. So, the preparation of the estimate was not money thrown away. If there had been no 'basis of credit', we wouldn't have been able to tell what half of it was, this being the sum of security, demonstrated by the sight of savings books of sufficient value.

I again borrowed five savings books kept under the mattress of my wife's friend, for one morning only. The society official looked at this proof of my good faith with great satisfaction. To show his trust, he asked:

"At what level of completion is the work just now?" adding: "Please don't say the tenth; the last tenth must be withheld until the borough council approves the building and issues the dwelling permit."

"It's the ninth," I replied. Whereupon the official, with one stroke of his pen, signed a draft for 108,000 forints.

I immediately squandered part of it on a new jeep, at 40,000 forints — just to prove my trustworthiness. Without transport, how could one ensure speedy completion?

Inspired by this ritual introduction to the mysteries of the state building society, my whole being was suffused by national pride. I concluded, with great satisfaction, that the richest and most farsighted financial institution in the world was financing our house. In a poor world there would be no credit, no loan, there being no security. In such an indigent world, there would be no reason to compel potential borrowers for credit to secure the money first, so that it could be lent to them — indeed, they wouldn't even know the purpose of credit.

By contrast, in a rich world there is so much security that there is little need for credit. Our world is halfway between the two.

The society, judging the security of the collateral to lie in people's determination to get money for building by hook or by crook, can invest its modest cash safely. It harnesses the strongest possible driving force: the scarcity of flats or houses. If someone wants to live in their own, they will find the money, to be sure. What more security do you need?

Part of the expenditure was thus assured by the building society loan. But our building programme envisaged a total expenditure of 5-600,000 forints, and on top of this there was repayment of the friendly loan for buying the plot.

I had few illusions about increasing my income as a translator. Even if I disregarded my daily bread (and that of my family) and devoted all my efforts to repayment of such a debt, I would have to translate about 160,000 pages. At a rate of 4-5 pages a day, that would mean a ten years' bondage.

To sell my father's town flat, worth about 300,000 forints, wouldn't have been enough — quite apart from the fact that it would have been bad business. I would only get money in exchange, less than enough — and money is depreciating all the time. Besides, this flat was the only collateral in hand during our search for the missing half million.

What is the sensible solution? To invest. At home or abroad. Unfortunately, that requires capital. Or something in lieu of capital... as long as it brings in some income. Capital could have been raised by selling my father's flat, but only a well-established enterprise, with increasing profits, could have ensured a sufficient and secure yield from 300,000 forints. Besides, since my friend had sold his flat speed was of the essence. There was not enough time to invest 300,000 forints safely.

The only capital that offered itself for suitable investment was my father! He was a surgeon, working in Nigeria. During his stay with us, he told us about the worries of Hungarian doctors and other medical personnel on contract overseas. These troubles struck a chord in our hearts.

Medics abroad get about three times their domestic salary. Half is creamed off by the state agency handling the export of their skills. The remainder is more than enough for a comfortable living. But while Hungarian scientific staff working in the U.S. or Western Europe can spend their surplus on travel, in Nigeria this is not advisable, politically and otherwise. They have a problem: what should they do with their money?

Simply remitting their currency earnings to Hungary would be suicidal, for obvious reasons. So I proposed a cure for the troubles of the staff in the expatriate hospital.

With a few exceptions — like my father who wielded his scalpel in the Third World in order to find an outlet for his oft-thwarted idealism — the majority of the hospital expatriates went to Africa for solid business reasons. There were no insurmountable barriers to their calculations, just a multitude of small ones. I sent my father a master plan for a single broad bridge over these barriers.

One pillar of the bridge rested on strict observance of the law, the other on the principle of better profits. The salaries of expatriate experts — more precisely, the share left untouched by the recruiting agency — paid in Nigerian naira, fell into two parts. One was for living expenses, the other for discretionary spending. They could not very well invest the latter locally, not for any ideological reasons, but owing to upsetting swings in white and black markets in Nigeria. So usually they invested their surplus in consumer goods that could be brought home. Most goods were obtainable in Nigeria — the problems lay not on the supply side but on the side of demand and profit-taking.

The best bargain for Hungarian expatriates used to be soap and razor blades: these ensured them an exchange rate of 200 forints against one pound sterling (the official rate was about 35 forints to the pound). But this necessitated bulk buying and transfer on such a scale that even the most tolerant customs officer was liable to raise objections, not to speak of completely upsetting the home market in these goods. Therefore — I wrote — expatriates should concentrate on commodities of smaller bulk, higher value, legally admitted, and should accept an exchange rate somewhat lower than 200 forints to the £. The nearer to 200 forints and the farther from smuggling, the better. He was to choose durables, which could be imported in any quantity.

In earlier days, customs authorities shackled the hands of citizens working abroad officially. Their purchases abroad had to be brought home in one lot, and were put under house arrest for several years. All purchases had to be declared and the goods were sealed and stored by customs until the owner could claim them for personal use, or prove their transfer by a bill of sale. If you brought home three washing machines, or five tape-recorders, you were in difficulties. The goods mouldered in a customs shed for years, the parcels disintegrated, and — adding insult to injury — the value of goods went down during storage. The 'importers' were frustrated, but so were those people who had been expecting their record-players, washing machines, TV sets, cars or whatever.

Somewhat belatedly it was recognised that the state should not send out its citizens for forced labour. There was no point in making their lives more difficult — or those of their friends, relatives and business associates. A few years ago, these awkward regulations were abolished. Now expatriates can mail home purchases, one by one. And they can be sold freely — although only after customs handling, which requires the presence of the owner. Until then, the goods can only be loaned. Once the owner comes back they re-borrow the car for a morning, take it to the customs, and the borrower can again drive the car in the afternoon, now a proud proprietor.

The regulations are not bad, but they need some refinement. Their effect is a temporary re-distribution of goods. With certain items, like a large car, there is no difficulty: it will roll on its own wheels between prospective buyer, real owner and customs official.

But if you invest in tape-recorders, videotape, record-players and the like — all promising better profits than a car — you would have to collect the lot for the day of the customs check. This might create problems of organisation, transport and accounting — sometimes even problems of ownership. There are fewer reliable friends than there are hi-fi units. While someone is industriously operating on appendixes abroad, he may neglect the bonds of friendship at home. Some emotionally neglected friend may then lose his sensitivity concerning ownership, and omit to return a 'borrowed' tape-recorder when asked to do so. This danger adversely influences the pattern of purchases, shifting it towards poorer profits or larger risks. The expatriate may be compelled to buy and resell a car at an exchange rate of 100 forints to the Pound, when on hi-fi equipment the rate would be 200 forints.

For unsentimental business one must find the right partners. Once we exclude smuggling, our search for supplies may be adversely affected. The most interesting items on offer in the bountiful markets of Africa will be ruled out if resale is limited to a circle of personally known buyers. The complicated system of lending and re-borrowing also tends to diminish the zest for entrepreneurship. And what price business without enterprise?

This factor also affects business acumen on the supply side. Western capitalists invest gingerly in Nigerian enterprises — the political situation is always a bit shaky, nationalisation might break out any time — and prefer to keep their funds in dollars. The same applies to Hungarian expatriates. But if Hungarian expatriates lose alertness and business sense, they may fail to build regular links with the Nigerian black market for currencies. Black market money-changers give a better rate than banks. Nigerian currency will inevitably end up in the hands of the black marketeer, owing to Western and Eastern caution. One result of this is that instead of large-scale industrial investment flourishing, commerce and black market do so. And thanks to the world export drive Western durables can be obtained more cheaply in Nigeria than in their countries of origin.

If circulation in the currency black market is too slow, expatriates only have to go on a shopping spree when their reserves are getting too big, or when they spot a bargain. Or they get to know the manager of a Western firm who is willing to charge them diplomat's prices.

The plan I put to my father in Nigeria aimed to solve these difficulties by creating a syndicate abroad and a distributive network at home. Once the balance of demand and sales was regularised and improved, this would benefit the supply side too. The plan was based on concentration of capital and rationalisation of the market.

The answer from Nigeria was an enthusiastic 'Yes'. The first condition of success was the establishment of orderly procedures, within the strictest legality. I began by eliminating all factors extraneous to the market. I had no use for tribal customs of trade prevailing before the creation of regular markets. There was no point in storing goods privately as a regular supply from Africa was assured. There was no need — in a developed economy — for an awkward system of lending and borrowing based on personal trust or uncertain exchange. The contingency of a personal network of friends and acquaintances had to be replaced by the more trustworthy state.

I asked customs headquarters whether there was any obstacle to state enterprises buying goods from Hungarian individuals working abroad. "None," was the reply. Once the expatriate returns permanently, and the goods are passed by customs, state firms could buy them as freely as private individuals.

This valuable piece of information immediately eclipsed the need for personal orders for tape-recorders, radios, toasters and so on in view of the very different demands of state concerns. Their currency allocation had been cut, but their craving for Western technical equipment had not diminished. The clumsy compensation deals they were allowed to arrange hardly satisfied their needs.

All these firms made stubborn efforts to keep up with their Western business partners. They felt they had to have equipment as good as that of their opposite numbers. It was also in their interest to spend up to cash limits, otherwise they might face lower cash allocations in future.

Of course, Western machinery — the symbol of increased efficiency — is not the only thing they want. Office administration has similar claims. The expatriates' revived business enthusiasm turned towards office equipment and allied technical items and away from hi-fi equipment and suchlike. According to the first findings of our joint marketing research, such items promised twice as much profit, including their gains at the currency market. The only drawback at the beginning was the fact that these purchases required larger funds than personal luxury items.

This was solved by the formation of a banking system, based

on proper dividends, by the Nigerian syndicate. My father was elected president, the matron became vice-president and chief cashier, the commercial department was led by the heart surgeon and a laboratory technician was appointed dispatch manager. A cardiologist was entrusted with accountancy and the most important department, the international credit division, was entrusted to the pathologist. The paid-up shares of these five members of the syndicate constituted the funds at the disposal of the chief cashier.

The dispatch manager's job was to approach expatriates about to return to Hungary permanently. Goods handed to them were nominally listed in their names, until they were passed by customs. The dispatcher was also in charge of advertising. She explained to the returnees how they could make two dollars out of one. One for themselves, one for the syndicate. The commercial manager also had two jobs: he accepted the orders from home and sought out the cheapest sources, preferably at wholesale or diplomatic prices. The chief accountant dealt with the distribution of dividends.

The founders of the syndicate put up the starting capital, and the returnees made up the fluctuating temporary membership, contributing the necessary funds on an *ad hoc* basis. At their board meetings the founder members approved the various deals, decided on purchases and shared the dividends on a pro rata basis. This beautiful theoretical model, of course, only came alive through the infusion of orders from the sales and distribution network in Hungary.

At first, I tried to build up this network on my own. A press photographer friend of mine ordered a Linhoff Technika camera, which soon arrived in the luggage of a urologist. However I now came up against the first obstacle: the official Sale-or-Return Agency, through which such deals had to be passed. The rate for the dollar at their price was no better than 50 forints. My friend would have been quite prepared to supply all his colleagues through my syndicate, but it seemed to me that there were some snags. The camera could have been sold at twice the price if it had not been for the annoying fact that press photographers travel abroad all the time. They receive a dollar allocation from which they buy their cameras and sell them officially to the sale-or-return agency. Then the newspapers which employ them buy the cameras, for the photographers who sold them in the first place. This was just a slightly more developed form of the barter trade I so studiously tried to avoid. The syndicate could have meant an easing of currency allocation to press photographers, but as this was not a very difficult barrier the prices they offered were rather low. It was not worth their while to pay more for the elimination of risk when — at a minimal hazard — they could buy cheaply.

Besides, the market in photographic equipment was not large enough. I would have had to find interested photographers, ask whether they wanted a new machine, find out whether their offices could pay for it and so on.

So I turned away from this market and tried another tack. This first poorish result had taught me to try to establish markets in goods which were more difficult to get. Without a more or less regular market, ready with money, there seemed little point in establishing a regular supply.

Having launched a marketing research effort, I soon picked up the first link in the chain, through the good offices of a friend who worked in a high technology equipment factory. He introduced me to their chief procurement officer. My friend assured me this man also had good contacts with buyers for other high technology firms.

At our first business meeting I learned that this industry had grave shortages and unlimited funds. Prospects looked bright. I gave up part of my commission and agreed with the chief buyer that he would get 10 per cent for every item sold through his efforts.

The first item the syndicate despatched for this new distribution network was a piece of electronic equipment — an oscilloscope. My purchasing officer friend produced the order from a company. This was sent to Nigeria and the machine flew in, this time in the luggage of a returning pediatrician. It cost $2,500 in Nigeria.

My new friend wanted to pass the order through the office equipment bureau where he had a friend who was one of the valuers. He thought that this way he could avoid splitting the commission.

His savings drive almost bankrupted the syndicate. When we appeared with the machine, we found that the buyer's friend had been promoted the week before, and an unknown valuer had taken his place. This man studied the invoice and technical details of the equipment and announced that he would not pay more than 40,000 forints for it, instead of the 200,000 we'd expected. He proudly declared that there was a perfectly satisfactory Hungarian-made oscilloscope which he recommended to Hungarian firms. The home-made unit cost 260,000 forints brand new, but he knew of little-used units at 100,000 forints — he would be glad to take an order for the company.

My friend argued in vain that his company would be prepared to buy the American oscilloscope for 250,000 forints. The valuer stuck to his guns. He could not understand why a company should buy a more expensive machine when a cheaper one was freely available.

"You have no regard for quality," my friend argued in vain. A failure so serious so soon could have led to the dissolution of the syndicate, and been a disaster for our house-building plans. My father had paid $1,300 towards the machine. The rest had been shared among the members, plus the pediatrician. After trying in vain to hawk the machine all over the town, my friend finally nailed the ex-valuer — now accounts manager — who agreed (for a consideration of 4,000 forints) to sort out the spoilsport valuer with a reprimand. Even so, we only got 180,000 forints for the oscilloscope, a rate of 72 forints to the dollar — far below the expectations I had raised in the syndicate.

I parted company with the buyer to stave off the anger of the syndicate board. A head had to fall and naturally it could not be mine. In the course of our attempts to get rid of the oscilloscope, I came across a new contact. True, I had got to know him through an ex-friend, but in the circumstances I had no compunction in cutting out the intermediary, and offered the new candidate the same terms as those offered to the failed buyer.

This new contact introduced himself as a purchasing officer, but in fact he was only stores manager at an office equipment distributor. Being smarter than many buyers he could easily manipulate the purchasing budget. As far as the company was concerned, it did not matter who spent the money, as long as it was spent. The obvious drive of this man seemed a better recommendation than the penny-pinching attitude of the former go-between. His business links extended far beyond office equipment. He came up with the idea of the IBM golf-ball typewriter, against my suggestion of a videotape machine.

I must explain that before this man joined our team, I had had a flash from the commercial manager in Nigeria, saying that videotape prices were falling sharply there. He could buy quite a few units if I gave him the green light. I called at the Sale-or-Return Agency (SoR) and was told that the sale price of a video was 460,000 forints. In Nigeria, it cost $1,900 — meaning a rate of 200 forints to the dollar. I hoped to restore the confidence of the syndicate, crumbling from failure with the camera and the oscilloscope, and wired the manager to send one unit to begin with.

The video unit arrived post haste with a homing rheumatologist. Following customs clearance, I rushed to the SoR. I had been so confident of the sale that I had promised the rheumatologist payment of his share that very day. But the SoR was chock full of videotapes. My new go-between explained that the videotape market had suddenly become saturated, and the SoR did not buy unlimited quantities for stock.

Just as it had been the thing for every company to employ a psychologist, a new fashion had meant that everyone wanted a videotape. From traffic controllers to science laboratories, every self-respecting outfit had to have a videotape machine. The sudden end of this bull market coincided with the slump in Nigeria.

Eventually it was the new link-man who saved my bacon. He found a sports club, sufficiently out of touch with fashion, willing to invest 460,000 forints in a video unit, hoping to ensure world fame for its members. Having produced a buyer, the SoR paid for the video, but my contact embargoed any further video sets and, instead, recommended the IBM typewriter.

This proposition promised a rate of only 100 forints to the dollar — half the videotape rate, but also half the risk. A balanced market in IBM typewriters seemed assured. Furthermore, the 100 forint-rate improved in the course of time. On every IBM machine there was, on average, an extra 20 forint profit, thanks to the set of spare parts. A typewriter costing $1,000 was accompanied by ribbons, golf-ball heads and other spares, to the tune of another $200. The SoR paid 1,000 forints for these.

Of course, the manufacturers only sold spares at these

favourable prices when they accompanied the typewriter — spares on their own were quite expensive in Nigeria too.

We thought we were in clover, when disaster struck again. IBM, probably unaware of our syndicate, entered into competition with us. They were planning to open a shop in Hungary and, as a bait, sent a large batch of cut-price ribbons and other spares. So we came a cropper with a fair quantity of our own spares: what had fetched 1,000 forints a week earlier (bought from us at 800) now slumped to 100 or 80 forints.

The loss of about 30,000 forints not only hit me but also the vice-president of the syndicate. It so happened that the matron fell in love with one of the doctors outside the syndicate. The whole expatriate community followed this romance with great sympathy. The doctor invested every penny he had in the syndicate, safe from the clutches of his wife. To help him, the dispatch manager had succeeded in getting more than one batch of spares with a typewriter. It was this very consignment that hit the rocks.

I desperately tried to make good the loss as the fate of the star-struck lovers was very much on my conscience. Before the foundation of the syndicate, the matron had bought an Akai tape-recorder — the type of which our new go-between so strongly disapproved, not wanting to chase private customers. The recorder had collected dust for a long time in the cupboard of the vice-president, so, in disgust, she dispatched it in the luggage of a returnee. The SoR price was about 20,000 forints, but they refused to buy it — the shop was as full of Akai recorders as of pocket calculators.

I had already half decided that, if all else failed, the Akai would have to be sold at a loss and I would bear this loss myself. Then, quite by chance, I spotted an identical model in the window of a suburban branch of the SoR, with a price tag of 30,000 forints. I went in and offered my unit for sale. Impossible, they said, the unit in the window had already been sitting there for at least six months. A few days later I walked past again and, lo and behold, the Akai had disappeared from the window. Apparently, somebody had bought it without shopping around. I went in again — still no deal, they said. Anyway, according to the current SoR price list, they could only pay 20,000 forints — the previous unit had been bought before the new list was issued.

Passing through the office, I walked around the shop. Two salesmen were in attendance. I approached the older one and asked him if he could find a way to flog the Akai at a higher price — it had customs clearance so everything was perfectly legal and above board. He was not interested, so I asked the younger one. This man knew of a potential buyer, but did not want to close the deal behind the back of the SoR, as the customer wanted to buy the machine on HP, using the facilities of the SoR. He made no promises, but asked me to look him up next time, and have the machine with me.

So I did, and the valuer in the office, who had refused my offer twice, burst into a warm appreciation of the advantages of the Akai, in contrast to Sony and the like — and offered me 28,000 forints, on sale-or-return terms.

On the way out I passed through the shop again and asked my young friend: how long? presenting him with a packet of Dunhill. He helped himself to a cigarette from behind two 100-forint notes, blew a ring and said: two weeks. Once there is a buyer, the store will not break the rules; indeed, for a prompt sale they get a pat on the back, in recognition of the higher turnover.

A fortnight later, I was asked to come for the money. I collected the 28,000 forints and left my friend a Dunhill packet lined this time with two 500-forint notes.

My go-between took care that I did not get in touch with the valuers and sales assistants of the SoR directly. Until IBM spoilt our plans by opening its own shop and forcing us to switch to another brand of typewriter, the balanced nature of demand and supply in the electric typewriter market made it unnecessary to bribe the valuers. The valuer only comes into play when he buys on sale-or-return terms or for stock. My friend brought a buyer for every machine and paid by cheque. For his 10 per cent commission, he assured the absence of risk to the syndicate, both legally and financially. Ensuring that sales and purchase happened at the same time he excluded the danger of price fluctuations between order and delivery. Once the buyer was willing to pay an agreed price, the SoR office concluded the transaction without further ado.

By making the deals official through the SoR, on the other hand, he guaranteed the legality of the affair. Private sellers lurking at the back door of the SoR either sell and buy among themselves, cutting out the valuer, or sell through the shop, bribing the valuer. Both methods are risky for all concerned, as this way they cut out the state from the profits. Whenever there is a drive against corruption, ther first target is the SoR and its environs, the tourists, with their smuggled digital watches, calculators and the like, or the valuers who buy these from them (for a consideration), although the stores are full of such items.

The deals of my go-between were always completely above board. The state also saved on scarce foreign currency, buying IBM or similar machines from the syndicate. The value of the Gross Domestic Product increased, as state companies were enabled to spend to the limits. The prestige of managers also grew, because their reports to the ministry, or their correspondence with foreign partners, were written on a golf-ball machine. And typists avoided the dangers of chronic inflammation of the wrist. The scope of business almost grew beyond the financial means of the syndicate.

(By studying the customs release notes of the returnees, I gained a good idea of the earnings of Hungarian expatriates. For example, one laboratory technician was obliged to wait two months longer than her contract period before a replacement arrived. This delay made it possible for her to buy a small Fiat car and a Sony hi-fi unit — over and above the usual goods.)

If the state had not taken away half the expatriates' salaries, they could have satisfied purchase orders placed by another branch of the state. I felt it would be beyond my rank and role to make suggestions in this direction. All I could do was to borrow the well-used arguments of the national economy and urge impatient companies, through the go-between, to be less greedy. At the same time, I encouraged the international credit division of the syndicate to greater boldness. It was difficult to do this across two continents and I could not go to Nigeria, as I was building my house.

The founder members of the syndicate were not prepared for this avalanche of demand. Owing to their previous lethargy, their links with the money-changers were still rather tenuous — the chief cashier was occasionally compelled to buy dollars from tourists for Nigerian naira: better than the bank but worse than the professional money-changers. The funds of the syndicate were never sufficient; after all, these were drawn from the earnings of salaried people. Membership also fluctuated. In the end, I had to make it clear to companies in Budapest that they should not expect the same prompt delivery as with their purchases paid for in hard currency.

In spite of these ups and downs, my father and I earned 475,000 forints in the first year. With a small contribution from my mother, this covered the building costs quite comfortably. The on-going business could safely be expected to pay for the original debt. In line with our separate private agreement, my father advanced his share towards the building costs, against my mortgaging to him my future dividends from the syndicate. As a matter of fact, my own dividends did not depend on any financial investment, only on my moral capital. In devising the syndicate, I could claim a kind of intellectual investment and the dividends due to this.

I also toyed with the idea that, in order to increase my moral capital by a more tangible asset, I should exchange the whole building society loan for dollars in the Hungarian black market and invest the dollars in Nigeria. This proposal would not have been incompatible with the presidential dignity of my father — indeed, it would probably have added to the respect the other members felt for him. However, the remnants of his erstwhile idealism morally forbade him to countenance my taking hard currency out of the Hungarian national economy. To induce me to drop this sensible — but in his eyes, morally reprehensible — suggestion, he offered me his first year's dividend. He felt it was wrong that I, a private citizen, should help the Third World by gradually shifting the building society loan to Nigeria.

This was a pity; my stance had indirectly been supported by the building society official who had pointed out to me that while I was building, the state did not remain idle either, as money lost its value and the only defence against this was investment. That would mean everyone profited; the building society, the state, the syndicate, myself. It would have been child's play to pass on the loan instalments to the mother of a colleague. She was receiving sizeable sums from New York regularly and could have easily switched the flow to Nigeria (at a rate of 30 forints to the dollar, instead of the official lower rate). I could have paid her the equivalent in forints.

This US contribution could have doubled the syndicate's funds earmarked for purchases; my father and I could have become majority shareholders; the income of all members could have been increased. My income would have soared, partly by purchasing certain items on my own account, partly through the growth of the total dividend, partly in fatter commissions.

From a short-sighted point of view it could have been said that the currency reserves of the National Bank might have been clipped somewhat, but this would have been balanced by the ever-increasing stock of Western equipment at national companies.

Alas, my father was still a prisoner of his scruples. Although by now he could see that our syndicate worked more productively than the national economy and actually benefited the country, he couldn't be budged. I had to respect his feelings and did not argue with him, even though I could have pointed to the clearest proof of preservation of assets: we had not had to sell my father's flat. He can retire there, and, like so many of his old comrades, write his memoirs about an ancient faith in what seemed to be a good cause.

3. The Work Begins

We did not have to start from the ground up: the foundations and main walls of the house were already there. Our first job was to put on the roof. This sequence — from the roof down to the ground — in a way mirrored the development from day-dreaming down to earth.

The roofing timber was all there, ready and waiting. The only snag was that it wasn't ours. The previous owner had bought it but hadn't paid for it. Now that we were friends again, he promised to let the rightful owner know.

This character turned up one day, and was rather put out to find new faces at the house. We had reckoned with his surprise; we wanted the timber, but he was in a cleft stick. If we offered less than he expected, finding a new customer and lugging the timber would involve him in a lot of extra expense, perhaps more than the extra profit he expected from the increase in price. He had bought the timber some time ago at the state fuel depot and there had been at least two price increases since. All he planned to do was pocket the difference at current prices.

That was the basis of our squeeze. He quoted a realistic price: we offered a ridiculous one. He left, gnashing his teeth. We waited and he reappeared, ready to pick up the timber. The haggling went on in front of the house. He reduced his price but we stuck to ours. We were waiting for the threshold below which the seller would not go. You can guess at this, you must work towards it. I'd learnt this method in the Istanbul bazaar a few years ago, on my way back from visiting my father in Africa.

When the seller lost his patience and told his men to start loading the timber, I paid his last price: 10,000 forints. We had been so confident of our bargaining powers that we had started putting up the roof.

The owner saved something by not transporting and storing the timber, and lost on the price increase. We saved a bit from the extra cost caused by creeping inflation. As it turned out, I could have bought the timber at half the final price, if I had let the man go with his goods. It was only later when I realised the true state of affairs that I saw there are ways and ways of buying timber — or anything else — and I'd chosen the wrong way. It had been a mistake to try and import the hallowed customs of the bazaar. I should have explored indigenous sales methods.

My partner, the practical man, took me first to the communal scrap yard — that's where one should begin, he said. We made a list of the things we needed and bought three buckets, a pulley and block, ropes, chisels, two spades, a pickaxe, a spirit level and a few pounds of nails for 500 forints. We couldn't think of anything else — how little we knew! Throughout the period of feverish negotiations and permit applications, we had been planning. Our favourite expression was: do it yourself! Once we'd got through the paperwork, we would do it all ourselves. Only when we got to fixing the pulley under the roof did we start to question what we meant by doing it ourselves.

I suppose we thought we would do the unskilled work ourselves but hire artisans for more tricky jobs. We assumed this might mean a lot of saving but had no idea how much. We made some inquiries in the neighbourhood and found we could expect to pay 40 forints an hour for unskilled labour. This was more than I could earn by translation, so I suspended my work in this line. My partner did not give up his job, but worked very hard in the evenings and at weekends.

If we could entice a crew engaged on someone else's job in employer's time, they'd cost us 30 forints an hour apiece. (This was so cheap that towards the end of the work we used this kind of unskilled labour: our own work was worth more than that.) If, on the other hand, a craftsman came along one weekend with a mate, that would cost at least 50 per hour: hence the 40 forints average. It seemed sensible, therefore, to learn some craft skills.

In the course of time, the 'do it yourself' concept blossomed in rich variations. My partner started with one advantage — being an engineer he could undertake all the electrical wiring. I learnt fairly quickly the simpler aspects of carpentry, bricklaying and eventually tiling.

As we progressed from the roof to the groundwork, I began to realise that using grey matter might be more fruitful than learning manual skills or even higher crafts. My partner may have saved 3,000 forints on the electrical work, while I, by going after contacts, getting useful inside information and the like (for instance, in picking up breeze-blocks, or unearthing a heating oil container) could save 40-50,000 forints for the partnership.

We'd decided at the very beginning that we would use moonlighters, not private sector artisans, and thereby save at least one small part of the cost: the tax to be paid by the private sector entrepreneur.

The difference between a private sector operator and a moonlighter is deep and significant. The private sector entrepreneur is fully licensed, has to render invoices and has to pay tax. The moonlighter is probably just as good at the job — maybe better — but keeps no records and doesn't pay any tax. They may, for instance, be a plumber at a state enterprise who comes along at weekends, gets paid but doesn't indulge in invoicing and suchlike. The lack of an invoice is no great loss, the building society doesn't insist on it. When we decided not to use private sector artisans, this wasn't just puritanical self-denial on our part. Over and above the saving of tax, we anticipated further cost-savings too. The private sector operator has to charge for purchasing and preparing materials and supplies, the time factor involved in getting and transporting these — if we were to do these things ourselves, we would be making a net gain (quite apart from the aggravation of the contractor skipping from one job to the next).

However, there is an even greater potential gain from the careful selection of a moonlighter. The real treasure is the one who brings supplies and materials from their regular workplace. A moonlighter of good standing might allow us to charge the most expensive items to the state entreprise — unofficially, of course. The private sector odd-jobber and moonlighter usually charge the same hourly fee — but the moonlighter doesn't have to chase items in short supply, doesn't have slip a few banknotes to the sales assistant, doesn't have to send calendars to the importer. All these are dealt with by an employer. It was the first moonlighter we'd engaged who opened up this splendid prospect, proving again that actual 'praxis' is worth more than the most elevated theoretical speculation.

We stood on the scaffolding, my partner and I, and had to admit that a carpenter was needed for lifting the roof. I had an actor friend who knew the head carpenter of his theatre. He came along, looked round, measured up the house, checked the material and declared: two carpenters were needed, provided we two carried the rafters. He could do it, he and his mate, for 12,000 forints. We said thanks for the estimate.

Naturally, we wanted to find out about prevailing prices. The father of my tennis partner used to be a carpenter, he said we shouldn't pay a penny over 8,000 forints.

I phoned the head carpenter and offered him 8,000 for the job. He thought it over and accepted. He didn't find anything unseemly in this haggling and we eventually became friends.

He and his mate worked from Friday afternoon to Monday midday. They brought with them a large circular saw from the theatre workshop without which they probably wouldn't have undertaken the job. Private sector carpenters can't usually afford such equipment. They use hand saws, which puts up their prices, for they take longer. Even run-of-the-mill moonlighters could only have afforded to do it if they had worked for us in their employer's time. The saw wasn't in use over the weekend and by bringing it, they could reduce working time by about a third, which made it possible for a further price cut of a fifth if need be. Those who cannot 'borrow' the state machinery 'borrow' their own paid working time.

8,000 forints seemed a realistic price for four days' work by two people, so everyone was happy. Later on, in our bargaining sessions with others, not knowing prevailing prices in their trades, we started by assessing the usual daily earnings of a skilled worker. Our top limit was 1,000 forints per day.

The price depends on several factors. For instance, who were the moonlighter's customers? Where did he live? Where did he work? Who were his relatives? And his former classmates? Our carpenter got his customers in and through the theatre. So he was spoilt: theatre people don't haggle. For highly-paid actors and producers, he was someone conveniently at hand, and that was that.

Our carpenter had an extra asset: his special skills acquired at the theatre. Other moonlighters or private sector artisans may have the same skills but can't use them. They find their customers among suburban tenants, poor relations, unsuccessful schoolfriends; they can't push their prices beyond the limits of their customers' purse, so they get used to this level. If they worked somewhere else, they could probably make better use of their skills, but they don't get the chance to venture farther afield: they have to knock up pantry shelves, carve legs for kitchen stools, glue on the broken arm of the Put-U-Up bed. All they can use their higher skills for is to construct the Houses of Parliament or the battleship Aurora from matchsticks, inside a Coca-Cola bottle.

Our carpenter worked at a place where his skills were at a premium. Among his specialities were spiral staircases. He designed my staircase too, at half the price quoted by a professional architect. He charged only 1,000 forints for it.

The next job, fixing the purlins, wasn't included in the 8,000 forints fee: we had to do it ourselves. We had learnt a few tricks of the trade from the carpenter in his four days, and the carpenter's mate stayed on to help us with the roof-tiling. I was standing on the rooftop hammering away — no small feat considering that in my childhood I'd suffered from vertigo, when the carpenter's mate suddenly said he would be willing to do the entire job for 3,000 forints. I almost fell off the roof and had to grab his hand, thereby closing the deal. Our neighbours had said it would cost at least twice as much: 28 forints per square yard, while my friend gave his hand on 17 forints for the same. He was a country boy, not used to the high prices prevailing in our area. He promised to come and do the job as soon as the plumber put up the guttering.

We had to find a plumber, double quick, before our friend got wise about town prices.

My mother knew a trade union official working in a borough building department. This acquaintance in turn knew of a plumber working for another borough council. I was rather reluctant to entrust the job to a plumber with an unknown background but the introduction seemed to ensure he wouldn't pull a fast one on us.

One afternoon I called at the departmental office, when the workmen were due to knock off. Around quarter to four, they started to filter in. I said to an office girl: "From the trade union", she gave me the name of the plumber and when he entered, she formally introduced us to one another.

"Get changed, I'll wait for you," I said. The girl whispered to him: "From the trade union." He seemed quite relieved. His relief turned into joy when I told him in the car that, far from being after him, I'd come to offer him some work. He was quite grateful that I'd been so circumspect at the office; and gave a price near on what we'd expected. He dictated a materials list and we had to promise that the galvanised sheets would be there within a week. He solemnly promised that he wouldn't keep us waiting with 10,000 forints' worth of material on our hands.

The plumber was a very nice man. One could see that he loved his trade and enjoyed his work. This good impression was mutual. No one could imagine at the time that this would be the cause of a disaster. In the end, this mutual empathy almost completely wrecked the drainage system — draining our pockets, that is.

The plumber started working like everybody else, with a will, in a thoroughly conscientious manner. We watched him, quite enraptured. When we saw how pleased he was by this attention, we discreetly withdrew and did something else. When the plumber noticed that we were not admiring him any longer, he lost his enthusiasm. He also discovered we didn't know a good plumbing job from a bad one. This made him downcast.

He had cut the yard-and-a-half long troughs required for the guttering from the galvanised sheets with the greatest care and artistic satisfaction. But when it came to assembling them, he made a mess of it and pocketed his cash anyway.

Six months later the rainwater, pouring down from the badly soldered joints, washed away whatever was left of our faith in human empathy.

Well before that downpour — the consequence of our own carelessness — we had to think about balancing the disadvantages of a moonlighter against the advantages. The moonlighter, unfortunately, gives no guarantees, while the licensed contractor, by issuing an invoice, does undertake some responsibility.

It took us quite a while to learn that there wasn't any guarantee of quality for our cash.

The buyer cannot compensate for lack of technical know-how with cash. The parties move in separate circles: the buyer in the circle of money, the artisan in the circle of his craft. And while the artisan can, in a manner of speaking, cross over to the buyer's circle and take the principal's money, the buyer cannot penetrate the magic boundaries of a trade with which they're unfamiliar.

There's nothing to compel a plumber to use good materials in places invisible to the uninitiated, when shoddy ones might do. Your artisan may confess to a few nasty tricks and demand more money for not applying them; but what's the guarantee there aren't others you don't know about?

Someone grown up in the good old days may suggest an appeal to pride in good workmanship. My young plumber would hardly listen: in his training course there was no subject called Pride or Honour. The prick of conscience doesn't trouble him. There may exist an immensely old owner (how on earth would he have funds for building?) who might, perchance, stumble upon an equally aged plumber who still believes in the sanctity of contract. For them, this common belief would serve as guarantee.

The plumber and I, we grew up without care for pride or honour. Our clue is Learning. Ours is an open society indeed: there's nothing to prevent me from learning all the tricks of trade, from plumbing to tiling, from bricklaying to central heating. Then I could check the work for myself. The snag is that though I might indeed become a jack-of-all-trades, the time spent learning would hardly leave me any time to practise my skills.

All this goes to prove that socialism is without a doubt a system superior to any previous one. By abolishing religious beliefs, the system has done away with such empty ideas as Pride or Honour. Socialism ensures that it's not such airy-fairy things as 'Sanctity of contract' that will protect the house-owner against his contractor, but personal relationships within society.

The system does not allow Things to get on top of People. Alienation will be banished. Money cannot buy quality — that would be capitalism. With us, human relations govern material ones. There must be a supervisor behind every worker: this is the only way to guarantee quality. Nothing else can ensure that people will do what they're supposed to do.

In this manner, socialism reifies all human failings, like cheating, falsehood, double-cross, negligence, superficiality. Humankind is the supreme value. We must put our trust in people, not things. We must realise that between the completion of work and payment due, there stands a person. The dissonance between the two aspects can only be resolved through personal relations. And as needs cannot always be satisfied with money, they cannot be alienated.

The attitude of the plumber to the guttering would be quite different if the person wanting a job done could help him get a car licence out of turn; or a passport; or extra pension years for his mother-in-law; or a patron to ensure his brother's university entrance. His little sister could perhaps be admitted to a better school; his brother-in-law could be helped in his application for a trade licence. He himself might fancy a season ticket to the university swimming pool. Or a permit to state hunting grounds. A civil engineer somewhere might divert a road, away from his holiday home.

The artisan can buy quite a lot of desirable things from high earnings, but far from everything. Their circle of relatives and acquaintances is different to that of customers. The different circles may or may not be on the same steps of the social scale. The artisan can amass almost limitless amounts of money by selling scarce labour power, as long as they have physical strength; but to *spend* money in line with growing ambitions, they need backers somewhere along the line. A buyer from another circle can compensate for this shortcoming. Someone of a higher social standing can enjoy certain privileges, due to status; such advantages cannot be had for money alone for someone lower on the social ladder.

Backdoor contacts and influence can be a much better guarantee for work properly done than money, for another reason too: money, once paid out, disappears without trace, while the benefit promised may take a long time to materialise, thanks to the workings of bureaucracy. There is a waiting list for a new car; the hunting licence also takes time; university entrance comes up next spring — and if rain pours down through the shoddily soldered joints of the guttering, it can wash away the goodwill necessary then.

The beauty of this linkage is that pride in good work does not disappear: it can be uplifted by suitably placed influence.

We gradually recognised this interaction. When it came to selecting the next worker, our aim was to find one dependent on someone else — like the private sector contractor, whose licence can be suspended by his trade association. In the case of the plumber, the dependence wasn't strong enough: a reprimand from the trade union doesn't frighten anyone.

At this stage, we required bricklayers for the dividing walls. In this instance, we committed a similar mistake in the short term; but what we learnt in the long term turned out to be infinitely more valuable than the cost of our error.

My tutor in this venture was an old party member. He used to work for an outfit directly controlled by the Hungarian Workers' Party. It was called Model Housing Office or something of the sort. I'd met him at the renovation of my mother's house, and we became quite friendly. He liked to tell long stories about his days in the erstwhile illegal Communist Youth Movement, to which I listened with great interest. He was very proud of being involved in the building of socialism — in his case, in its literal sense. He built almost exclusively for leading comrades. Once, however, socialism reached our highly developed stage, he promoted — according to the laws of marxist dialectics — a qualitative change: he became a private sector building contractor.

Whenever we met in the course of the years, he always had a cheery wave for me; now he received me at the gate of his residence with a Brezhnev-like hug. Passing his garage, I saw there was not one Mercedes car but two.

Sitting on his terrace, with coffee and drinks, it became clear soon enough that we couldn't have his bricklayers — they were booked up for months, and they were too pricey for me anyway. What he offered me was worth far more: valuable information.

He'd started life as an ordinary bricklayer. As a good party member, he'd been sent to an evening course and obtained his engineering diploma. He'd been appointed group leader at the party building office I'd mentioned. This worked exclusively for leading party members, among whom he was very popular. While his team was engaged in building a town house for a party notable, my friend could not refuse a request to rebuild the cellars in this comrade's vineyard.

While he was working there — not officially, mind you, just with a few helpers — it so happened that the chairman of the local council called on him. This official could have used the local builder to put up his family tomb, but it was to his advantage — more than the price difference — to be on good terms with a builder working in the vineyard of a leading comrade from the capital. This offered a useful way to the ear of the party official — through the builder, he could glean information about village problems — how far they had got with the paved road; how much would be needed over and above the council budget in order to bring the sewage or electricity as far as the comrade's vineyard. So it was in the party bigwig's interest to phone the local deputy in Budapest and say a good word about village development.

The council chairman would be reimbursed for the difference between the cost of the local builder and the city builder somehow; after all he served the interests of the whole village. Once the local agricultural co-operative got wind of the matter, it might decide to increase its contribution to the village budget, in the hope that the deputy would use his good offices to boost the state subsidy to the county. This might mean more and better roads, more bus lines; the flight from the land might ease. With a more stable labour force, the co-op could realise its cherished plan for a chicken hatchery. This would raise the level of incomes all round; besides, a higher budget would improve the image of the co-op and of the council no end. Then the grateful populace would re-elect the leadership, thereby strengthening the basis of its long-term privileges.

My friend's role was similar to that of a minister's chauffeur, with the important difference that he could serve not only the interests of his birthplace, as the driver did, but of as many villages as happened to harbour hunting lodges, vineyards and holiday homes of the great and the good.

Times have changed: now it's not the party that is erecting houses for its leaders; they do it on their own account. It's still he who builds them, now in his capacity as independent contractor. Apart from party notables and high government officials, he had also acquired a wide range of customers, all impressed by his inside stories and hints of exalted connections. I saw bookings two years ahead on his desk.

He picked out F's name from his address book, saying he was a friend and would be my friend too. This remark was accompanied by a broad wink. F was the foreman at one of the state building enterprises; he offered himself and his brigade leader for the job, at a pretty stiff price. Gazing at the healthy pink of their hands there in the office, I would have bet anything that they hadn't touched a trowel for the last 20 years. Why had my old friend recommended these two characters? What was the meaning of his wink? I put my trust in good old party traditions and expected a miracle.

Not so my partner who, looking at those rosy hands, was very put out. When he saw the first crooked wall, he blew his top. It was a miracle that the wall didn't crumble there and then. The incompetence of the two so-called bricklayers was so obvious that I had to think again about the significance of that wink. After all, why should my friend want to do the dirty on me? I may not belong to the select circle which was the source of his popularity, but I was at least on the fringe of it. Something started to stir at the back of my mind when F and his mate made the first feeble moves at plastering the wall. They could hardly get the scaffolding up, the wall was so crooked.

The scaffolding! That was it... that was what my friend had been hinting at! They had brought an awful lot scaffolding. They assured me we would need loads and loads of scaffolding. One could have assumed that eventually they would take it away

— but that was not their intention. In fact, F and his mate were materials suppliers. They supplied my friend with all the stuff he needed... from the state building enterprise. In exchange, my friend secured other outlets for them — like ourselves. The bricklaying was just an excuse, only we were too dense to see through it.

In fact, I was only an extra in this stately ballet; my friend had been hinting that it was up to me to become a leading actor.

Entering into the spirit of the scenario, I tried to make good my original blunder. The dialogue of the play had been strange to me and I hadn't understood the prompter at first. So I bought 2½ cubic metres of first-class board for 7,500 forints — at the building centre (if available) it would have cost 15,000 forints. Then I bought 2½ cubic metres of seconds, for 4,500 forints; official price 12,000 forints. I now had at least three times as much as we needed for our house. So I graciously passed on the surplus to a needy neighbour, at somewhat less than official prices.

I must stress that I didn't shortchange F and his mate. On the contrary. They're taking the same risk loading a lorry with state property whether they fill it to capacity or not. The heavier the load, the greater their earnings. Finding the customer is the real skill.

In the end, we got our timber for nothing, and the sale of the surplus enabled us to pick and choose real bricklayers.

Now that I was moving confidently on the stage, I began to understand and enjoy the little games going on throughout the neighbourhood. Once I went round to pick up a few clamps and whom should I see, busily knocking down an old shack? My friend the venerable council official, demolishing walls for 70 forints an hour. At another plot, the chief inspector of the electricity board was the mate of a moonlighting electrician. No doubt for a similar wage, he being a first-class expert.

It's not always possible, and may not be worthwhile, to corrupt someone at their place of work. But if the would-be builder — instead of vainly arguing over plans — happens to mention they're in need of a skilled labourer, the architect may not leave their desk immediately, but, by strange chance, turn up at the building plot on a Saturday afternoon. Another customer may find that an irregular building plan will be put right by a friendly council official physically laying down the concrete in the proper manner.

How much can a penpusher earn at the office? Not more than 3,500 forints, with maximum overtime. If they're prepared to spend summer weekends demolishing walls, they can earn 5,600 forints — 10 hours a day at 70 forints per hour. Supposing someone tried to bribe them. They might be slipped a thousand-forint note at most. And wielding a pickaxe also provides exercise for sedentary occupations. If they are too tired (or less proud than the council official) they can still pocket the envelope. The choice is theirs.

For the owner it's all the same, a white collar labourer for a high wage or blue collar for less. Similarly, the electrician could find a cheaper mate than the inspector. But with this accomplished expert in a humble role once in a while, the inspector — or a colleague — may happen to pass a wiring not exactly conforming to the strict standards laid down in the book; thereby paying for the higher wage, quite apart from the fact that proper wiring materials can't be had for love or money.

It was time to re-assess the art of hiring moonlighters. Now, if I need a carpenter, I jump in my car and drive slowly round state building sites. The carpenters are there, resting on the beams... and so are bricklayers, plumbers, electricians — one only has to whistle and they come. If not at once, then next day, or at worst the following weekend. At first we were a bit embarrassed, but we soon found out that anybody could join in. There are no fixed roles or rules — it's a democratic game, there's no snobbery of expertise in it. One can, of course, play the game in an exclusive manner — with the friend of a friend — behind closed doors, but what's the point? Isn't a popular, collective game more fun — after all, everyone may have some hidden talent for it. It calls for spontaneous creativity. Indeed, it's the ultimate in 'do it yourself'. The name of the game is, of course, the state building programme — and everybody plays it according to their own wits.

This programme is so successful that it is carried on, year after year. New entrants to the game are all those who have a justified claim to a council flat. Their numbers are increasing apace, as all those who couldn't get a flat last year are joined by those who have only just got on the waiting list. The game is based on the fact that there are never enough flats or houses. The continuation of the game is ensured by the conditions entitling one to a council flat: your social situation. What else? After all, this is a socialist society, not a capitalist one — it is governed by social need, not money.

Elsewhere, where money is the governing principle, the state is a minor factor in house-building. Those who have the money will build or buy for themselves. The state only intervenes where it is compelled to: it builds roads, schools, hospitals, paid for by taxation. This is called social policy; but economic life, the business world, is left to its own devices.

In our kind of society, the state is doing much more than that. It does build roads, schools, hospitals, nurseries, houses but, in addition, it also organises and directs the whole of economic life. People are, therefore, grateful to the state, they appreciate that the state carries all these burdens for them, so they are eager to help in sharing the burden. They don't just wait passively until social policy allocates them a flat. But how can they help the success of social policies? Not directly, not by money — that would be the capitalist road.

What is the main problem of our economy? The shortage of labour. That's where all these helpful people can come to the aid of the party: they rush off in all directions and build their own houses with their own two hands. Council houses are also short on quality. These busy people make up for this and build quality into their own houses.

Shortage of materials is less of a problem. Seeing this tremendous goodwill, the state building industry puts all the stuff required in these outstretched hands: bricks, beams, boards, nails, whatever. It helps with transport too, utilising equally helpful moonlighters. Indeed, the state enjoys moral gratification, seeing how industrious its citizens are. Both state and citizens proclaim thus the sanctity of work.

The state asks itself: how can one help all these busy people? What is plentiful? Goodwill is plentiful. So the state benevolently overlooks the activities of stores' supervisors, it mollifies the disciplinary inclinations of foremen or brigade leaders. After all, by sharing this economic burden, citizens undertake a good part of the whole housing policy, they also mitigate the headaches of materials distribution: there are fewer refusals of proper claims

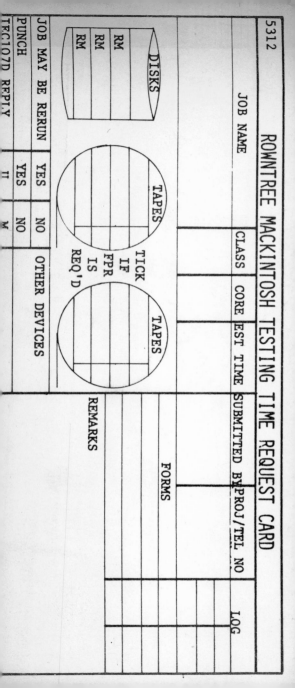

P. 50   Reifies
         Dissonance

and more people have a house to live in.

Let us assume that the state could and would carry out the whole house-building programme. Surely, all the houses would be more expensive. All those on the waiting list — obviously, socially disadvantaged people — would have to pay the difference for *not* carrying away all those bricks, beams, boards and so on, *not* enticing moonlighters in employer's time, and thereby painfully re-establishing economic efficiency at state enterprises.

Why should the state punish its own helpful citizens? In fact, it gives them a helping hand. All those entitled to housing take into their own hands the distribution of supplies, thereby contributing valuably to the governance of the economy. No capitalist or bureaucrat can stand between the state and its grateful citizens.

That's why we must not allow the state to wither away. It's the only one we have. And if there were no such thing as the state, it would have to be invented.

4. Transport

Hiring a moonlighter and getting supplies are two games subject to the same rules. The link between them is transport. The closer the link, the cheaper the deal.

To enable F and his mate to do their botched job, we needed bricks. Also mortar. For the mortar, they needed cement, lime and sand, quite a lot of it. I found out a funny thing, long after the house was almost complete: you can buy the sand openly and legally, and get it delivered. It's there, writ large on the posters of the Forestry Products Company. I don't think many people have noticed it. I suppose it's because Forestry Products conjures up the idea of raspberries or blackberries, not sand. And it's quite a bargain: 750 forints the lorryload, delivered, instead of 1,400 forints from a 'black' lorry.

What complicates things is that the building centre also sells sand, but doesn't deliver it. So 'black' sand has become so much the rule that no one thinks about the cheaper above-board supply.

I found this out in a roundabout way: I called at the forestry shop for fishing bait. That's where I saw the advertisement. Of course those who are engaged in building would hardly have the time for weekend fishing. Most people work like slaves over Saturday and Sunday; and have to rest at their workplace during the week — or, if they can slope off, rush around getting transport for the materials needed for the following weekend. For those in the know, there are the 'black' drivers. Sensible people buy the sand from them, to save time and trouble. So 'black' drivers can charge more than the official price — while the cheaper sand of Forestry Products goes begging.

Before the arrival of F and his mate, I posted myself at the (long vanished) tollgate on a main road. I waved down the first dumper lorry going outwards. "Er... sand," I said. The driver pulled me in next to him without any further ado.

"I haven't got the time just now," he said, "but I'll take you to the rubbish dump. There are plenty of lorries waiting there. They'll take you to the diggings."

At the dump, I flagged down the first lorry available, and we sped off to the quarry.

Six hundred, ventured the driver. Four hundred, was my reply.

"Hell, no one else would do it for that," he grumbled.

He was down and out, that lad. It was the only time I managed to beat down the usual price. My friend had just come out of jail and badly needed some cash. He was twenty-three but had already spent five years behind bars. He had been sentenced eight times, invariably for grievous bodily harm. He lived with his parents, seven people sharing two rooms. When he wanted some relief from overcrowding, he went down to the local. Whenever there was a punch-up, he joined in. The last time he was quite innocent — self-defence, he said. Of course, after seven previous offences nobody asked him how he'd got into the punch-up. When the fuzz arrived, they gave him the beating of his life, then he was put away for eight months.

While we were driving along, he explained the routine of sandbagging. I needed only three cubic yards; the mechanical grab automatically loaded four, to capacity. That was 50 forints to the operator. At the gate, the gatekeeper took the ticket you'd borrowed from the driver and, pocketing 20 forints, returned it to the driver on the other side. It's a well-oiled routine. In truth, I was particularly lucky to hit upon this poor devil. Usually there's no mention of price. You're just asked: "Where to?" When it's delivered one just passes on the usual. I tried it on once, and gave a driver less than the usual: his honest indignation was a wonder to behold. After that I used his expletives when another driver tried to demand more than the usual from me.

If I stop a lorry and the driver actually mentions a price, I just send him off — it means he wants to waive the rules. Most of them stick to the usual. Normally, I wave down a lorry: I want some sand. The answer is either yes or no, depending on the driver's line. Let's say I stop a lorry belonging to an aluminium factory: he carries tubing and pipes, not sand. If it's a builders' lorry, there will be sand. Or something else. Each driver has a number of well-established sources; the 'black' delivery is part and parcel of his normal earnings.

Next time I needed sand, the driver took me not to the back of beyond, but to the nearest building site. It happened to be the new Metro, but could have been any new estate, underpass or whatever. These are as good as a natural sand digging. Thousands of cubic metres of sand are stored at such places and there is constant coming and going of lorries. The grab-man doesn't mind whose lorry it is, as long as he pockets his 100 forints for a large lorry, 50 forints for a small one. You only have to go out to the digging when the bricklayer wants some special sand. So it's advisable to agree with the driver on the quality of sand you need, otherwise you may end up sieving the stuff all day at the site. Sand used for ballast is no good for mortar. Whenever I'd agreed in advance, I was never cheated.

Nine tenths of lorry drivers belong to a semi-secret guild (the rest are cowboys). I don't know exactly what risks they run. In the case of sand deliveries, it is very important to have a ticket for the stuff: black haulage is a venial sin, but theft is serious. If a driver with a ticket for the goods is caught out without a waybill, the company may be notified and he may get a reprimand — whether severe or friendly depends on the company's complement of drivers. But if there is neither waybill, nor ticket, that counts as theft. So most drivers have dozens of tickets for sand — building units get them in bulk. My friend had a nice collection too, although he had only been back in the trade for a few weeks. Maybe the guild had helped him out with donations. I was sorry I had no ticket of my own. I could have given it to him, to make up for his lower price; but then I would have had to queue for the ticket.

The reason why 'black' haulage is looked upon with such forbearance is the shortage of drivers. Since the bulk of freight goes by road, it is in every company's interest not to have its lorries standing idle in the yard. If a driver is fired for 'black' haulage, the lorry will be out of work until a new driver arrives. It's in the joint interest of all companies to keep the lorries moving, seeing that they are powerless against the guild.

So, if 'black' haulage is tolerated, the likelihood of idle lorries is reduced. Besides, through this accommodation the company safeguards itself against having to hire a driver who had been dismissed for theft. Sometimes they can't help doing this: when finished goods are piling up in the stores. If, however, a driver is caught stealing, the police have to start an investigation; whereas a report of 'black' haulage is an internal company matter, and it may or may not land in the wastepaper-basket.

If it is a police matter, detectives may call at the office, they may want to study the waybills, job cards, stock records; the driver's superiors may also get involved. If the police have more than one thieving driver from the same company, they may even order the production of protocols relating to previous reports on black haulage as well, with unforeseeable consequences. Therefore, it is in the company's interest to behave tolerantly towards its drivers, otherwise it may expose itself to unwelcome inquiries beyond its control.

This is not the only reason why companies are well advised to co-operate, in an orderly manner, with the drivers' guild. Driving lorries is a hellish job. Wretched roads, too many private cars, constant traffic jams, poor maintenance, lack of spares — the driver's working day is a hard one. They may not have fixed working hours, or, if they do, they constantly break the rules, for the sake of the company's business or their own. Maybe their lorry breaks down, they can't get a breakdown van, or find themselves miles from a service station or can't get the spare part they need. They usually work a 14-16 hour day.

No one can pay for this adequately, and, because of salary regulations, no one is allowed to. Nobody's allowed to pay 10,000 forints to a driver — that's a director's salary. But they have to. Below 8,000 forints, you wouldn't find a monkey to sit in the driving seat.

Ever since we'd started on the house I hadn't stopped once at a petrol pump. I got the fuel from lorry-drivers; one could regard them as mobile petrol pumps. Super grade is 15 forints per gallon. The company may pay them 4,000 forints, not more — but it can also give them twice the amount of fuel the lorry requires. No rule against that. What the drivers lose in miserly wages, they gain on the swings of freely flowing fuel. The lax control over 'black' haulage ensures this delicate balance is maintained.

This way the driver can make 10,000 forints a month on average, which is not over-generous but acceptable. Drivers can do what they like with the extra petrol: they can use it for carrying 'black' stuff ('investing' the fuel, so to speak — profit will be the amount charged for carriage) or can sell it off piecemeal to private motorists.

Drivers employed by large companies usually get their fuel at the company's own pump. Drivers of smaller companies are supplied with petrol coupons. The black market price of a coupon is 18 forints. So they can either sell the petrol in kind, or sell the coupon. On the face of it, the coupon business seems the better one, at 3 forints extra. However, if they use the petrol for 'black' haulage, there may be a greater profit in the long run. Apart from sand — which has a stable market price — the driver can do individual deals, depending on the nature of goods and the risks involved.

Some drivers go for the quick cash and sell petrol or coupons; some are just modest people, satisfied with a small profit. Others 'invest' the fuel, carrying sand, beams, scaffolding or pipes.

Another category is satisfied with the premium some concerns pay for fuel saving. This is always less than the riskier gain, but many people opt for the quiet life. There are spiritual satisfactions too, not just material ones. Otherwise why would anyone want to join the ambulance service?

Of course, such people may just enjoy fast driving. The

papers sometimes report hair-raising cases of speeding ambulance drivers; on the other hand, there have been cases of victims dying in the ambulance, because the driver was watching the fuel gauge, thinking of the premium on petrol saving.

It's a shade better in the fire brigade, where speeding is a social virtue, so the service attracts speed merchants with a highly developed social conscience. The only snag is that fire engines are mostly about 20 years old, hardly suitable for aspiring speed merchants.

It's difficult to renew all the old engines at the same time; it's easier for the fire chief to acquire a brand new command car — so their drivers can rush ahead to the scene of the fire. True, they can't do much before the arrival of the engines, but at least they can soothe the victims. The number of commanders is on the increase, so they can't all squeeze into the command car — so the command car is nowadays usually followed by a jeep with future fire chiefs, who may even carry a few buckets with them. Sooner or later there will be more jeeps, more buckets and they may even start fighting the fires before the engines arrive.

It stands to reason, therefore, that only drivers with higher social motivation join the ambulance service or the fire brigade. Otherwise why should they work for the worst pay, if not for the privilege of do-gooding? Of course, there may be less elevated but more realistic reasons: there may be few other jobs available. The same applies to the railways: in the old days, it was the prospect of a state pension that gave unique prestige to the job (and kept salaries low). Who cares about a pension nowadays? The railways recruit only those who happen to live in a poorly industrialised part of the country, where there is no other job on offer for people who want to leave the ranks of the vanishing peasantry.

In the capital, social motivation is decreasing in line with the increase in prices of desirable goods. Most drivers are ambitious people, so they sell the petrol, the coupon or the opportunity for moonlighting.

There is a well-established system in this black market, based on the scale of risk and the opportunities of 'black' business. Some drivers don't use their coupons on their own account and simply sell them to the petrol pump attendant. This is a steady business, with low risk and low profits. Profits can only grow in line with the increase in official petrol prices. Of course, this goes on all the time and there is no extra risk involved. The customers are mostly regulars, although one never knows whether, among new buyers, there isn't an inspector. That may be one reason why drivers who get the fuel at the company's pump prefer to use the petrol for 'black' haulage: the risk is the same but the chance of profit much higher. Of course, the inspector may appear in the guise of a customer for transport, not just for petrol, but that amounts to the same risk.

There is also a third way, for those drivers who for one reason or another have no regular customers and don't want to run high risks. Between 'white' and 'black', there is also 'grey' haulage. Here the risk is, in a manner of speaking, passed back to the company. In 'black' carriage, there are no names mentioned, whereas in 'grey' haulage, there is a bit of phoney paperwork. The driver gets paid overtime for fictitious drops, he can draw extra fuel — to be siphoned off into the sewer, so that next day he can claim again the extra quantity; besides, there will be no discrepancy between the phoney mileage on the clock and the fuel gauge. And the next day, he might pick up a *bona fide* buyer.

The first time I came across this phenomenon I thought the driver wanted a piss when he drove off the main road and stopped between two 6 ft-high maize plantations.

"In Brazil," he explained, "they dump coffee into the sea when they have more than they need. Here we do it with petrol, see?"

Which goes to show that rich countries aren't the only ones that indulge a passion for wastefulness. I had been doubtful when our leading economists had assured us that the oil crisis would not affect us. This driver's example justifies their assurance. There might be members of the drivers' guild who — with a higher moralistic sensitivity — would condemn such waste. But this kind of 'grey' manipulation safeguards the driver against the occasional tightening-up of control, so the majority understands, indeed often applies the technique. Why take unnecessary risks?

The free market for petrol operates in much the same way as it's bought by private motorists, at a fixed price. It would, however, be too obvious (and too dangerous) to flag down drivers on busy main roads. The driver mostly stops in a secluded place, siphons off the fuel into a can and hands the can to a go-between — a relative, friend, or pump attendant. Motorists usually buy from these, at 15 forints a gallon, considering that they too shoulder some of the risk. I do the same, calling at garages where I know the attendant; it's the same price as at the 'mobile pump' (the drivers contribute to the overheads of the go-between).

The heavy lorries run on diesel oil, not petrol. The buyers for diesel oil are not motorists, but those who use it for central heating. Therefore the price varies according to season: throughout the winter, it is 7 forints per gallon, come spring, it drops to 4. This price fluctuation also explains the apparent perversity of 'grey' drivers in draining off the fuel: it's not always easy to find a buyer for 70 gallons of diesel oil in one go.

Needless to say, there are quite a few enterprising garage owners who maintain a regular 'black' pump for heavy fuel. Provided they have a number of regular suppliers, and thus the security of an even flow, the garage manager will probably do better to buy additional storage tanks than to keep hidden earnings idle in a piggy-bank. What's left in the piggy-bank may be used next year for purchasing new supplies of heating oil at lower summer prices.

Petrol coupons, as I said, are somewhat dearer. As long as drivers and pump attendants play the game according to the rules dictated by the mechanism of the pump itself, there's hardly any risk. As we know, the pump works by turning the wheels both of the quantity gauge and the price indicator. The money should tally with the quantity, at the fixed price, of 20 forints per gallon when the attendant knocks off at the end of a shift. However, the money is made up of cash plus coupons. Now if the attendants pumped out 1,000 gallons, they will have to account for 20,000 forints; having bought the coupons at 18 forints each, they can pocket 2,000 forints clear profit. Of course, it is much more than a mere 1,000 gallons a day, especially in summer when the tourist trade picks up. As long as they are careful and don't try to flog too many coupons — foreign tourists pay in cash anyway — they can keep the ratio of cash and coupons to manageable proportions.

Unfortunately, even this trade is not safe from seasonal

fluctuations. In winter, many private motorists lay up their cars and there are fewer foreign tourists, so the chances for those on the make are that much worse, while lorry transport fluctuates less and guarantees a steady supply of coupons. You can't just hand in coupons and no cash.

That's when some reckless pump attendants may resort to desperate strategems. They tamper with the pump mechanisms. This may be discovered by the maintenance staff, who then demand a cut of the profits.

The pipeline-complex of petrol pumps is almost too intricate for the human imagination. While I was accompanying one driver after another on my expeditions for sand, timber and so on, they related a perfect whodunit: How had a complete tankerload of petrol disappeared from the Danube harbour into the pipeline of garages? The police were as baffled as the newspapers.

There is a sound balance between the attitude of companies suffering from labour shortage and the interests of the drivers' guild. The extra fuel ration, used for 'black' haulage, is the fulcrum of the balance. The system of mutual advantage and tolerance reduces the need for theft. Once a driver can make up to 10,000 forints per month on sidelines, to make a further 2-3,000 would increase the risks out of all proportion. In the long run it is worth while sticking to the rules: sooner or later, a thief will come a cropper. This unspoken accord between company and guild gives rise to certain norms of behaviour; this, in turn, affords some protection to the operators.

As in many fields, there are sinister gangs operating in transport, usually shunned both by companies and guild members. For instance, there are the taxi-vans lurking around furniture stores. They reckon that someone who's paid 30,000 forints for a drawing-room suite won't mind paying 500 forints to get it home instead of 120, the legal fare. These marauders live by the laws of the wolf-pack: if any outsiders venture near their hunting grounds, they tear them to pieces. Once I picked up a taxi-van further out. The driver was really scared, but as I was with him, it looked like a pre-booking, and the wolves left him in peace. He brought me and my purchase home for 120 forints plus the usual 50 forints tip. On another occasion, I was in a hurry and whistled up one of the predators who, of course, asked 500. But I did the dirty on him: being taller and stronger than him, I told him he'd get the regular fare and his tip — and if he didn't like it, he could go to the police. Gnashing his fangs, he left.

These carnivores are, however, the exception. Most drivers are honest, working to a well-established price list, within the rules of their own moral universe. They don't want to upset the market by undercutting one another's prices. Once a guild member agrees to deliver a lorryload of bricks for 600 forints, that's 600, not a penny more, not a penny less. This is simple self-preservation: if a driver were too greedy and tried to over-charge, they might come across a customer — like myself — who knows the going rate and find themselves facing the police. Sometimes it's the guild members who grass on a cowboy. But the one arrested could involve others. It's better to stick to the rules and not jeopardise the common interests of the guild. Moral in-dignation equals self-defence. Safety first, is their motto: after all, most drivers are decent people, with hungry mouths at home. Their pay slip only supplies half of the necessary; the other half is guaranteed by the guild, more effectively than by any trade union.

The guild's self-defence mechanism, as a barometer in-dicating supply and demand levels, offers a marketing research function more sensitive than any scientific approach. And the system of 'black' haulage acts as a regulator for official carriage charges. Official haulage enjoys a very high level of state sub-sidy. If it were withdrawn, all would-be builders would have to turn to the black market. Drivers would have no time left for business deliveries; public building works would slow down. Companies would be unable to complete their annual plans; people on the waiting list would have to start on their own houses, thereby increasing further the pressure on 'black' haulage. If the black market were to be abolished by increasing the subsidy even further (this is logically possible but in practice out of the question), everybody would lay siege to the haulage companies and there would be no time left for deliveries to state building sites. Tightening up on the black market would have the same effect; besides, everybody would be feverishly looking for new dodges, also taking up an awful lot of time — chaos and confusion would reign supreme.

Clearly, 'black' haulage is the optimal solution. Look at it from another point of view. Let's assume the opposite of 'black' is 'white'. 'White' in this sense means that something is — or is not — available. Official, I mean. I can always go to the building centre and queue up for a sand ticket. The tickets are always available. Next, I can go to a state haulage firm and pay in advance for delivery of the sand. With luck, within a few weeks the two pieces of paper meet and the sand will arrive; my walls can be put up. Once the walls are standing, I can go to the heating centre and book the central heating. The fitters are there, my order is booked; within six months or a year, the fitters arrive.

'White' therefore means that something is available, only you have to wait for it. The sand doesn't coincide with the bricklayer, nor does the fitter come when the walls are up. They may come sooner, they may come later. 'White' requires time and patience. If my time costs money, I'll try to reduce this cost. Analysing the composition of 'white', I find that it has a delicate shading. Purchase orders are scheduled by date order; outstanding orders are gradually dealt with; at one stage they may be left with two hundred orders but only one hundred lorries.

The integrity of the 'white' has now begun to fall apart. The dividing lines between availability and non-availability have become blurred. Black spots have appeared on the white, each one meaning that the gap between availability and non-availability has been narrowed. They have their origin in the fact that somewhere there is something of which there is none... Blackest black is sand in the quarry; greyish when it's at the site of the Underground; almost white when the two concepts of 'there is' and 'there is not', availability and non-availability, meet with the unloading of the sand at my house. The greater the number of black spots on the canvas, the narrower the gap between availability and non-availability.

If I leave the queue, I relieve the officials of one more file, I shorten the waiting time for others. Time is money: saving time doesn't always mean saving money, but never mind, it's still a good bargain.

Beginners tend to see things in pure white: what they need is there, it's required here — the route between the two seems straight as an arrow. They think the black market moves in strange ways. I have learnt that the ways of the black market are the straightforward ones, while the 'white' way twists and turns. Of course, one need not paint the whole picture black; that would be too frightening. One must use artistic freedom, juggle with complementary colours, apply delicate transitional pastel shades — not sharp contrasts. Black-and-white crudities are better left to sociologists.

My education continued with bricks. When you are paying a moonlighter, as well as yourself, reliable delivery is essential. In the building season, it's rather difficult to secure a 'black' lorry for a whole day; besides, this is far too expensive, perhaps twice as much as the charge for official haulage.

Bricks are one item to which the previous analysis applies: now you see them, now you don't. You can have them at the building centre (sometimes) at a hefty price: one has to pay for the transport between the brick yards and the centre, plus a percentage for storage, plus the overheads of the centre. At the yard, bricks are 20 per cent cheaper, but not always available. After considerable argument, we set up a new equation; namely some string-pulling + some 'black' haulage = bricks.

The end of the string was in the hands of my mother-in-law. She is in charge of the nursery at a large firm; one of the children in her care is the daughter of the head of the transport department. My mother-in-law knew that one of his subordinates, a lorry dispatcher, was nagging his boss for a nursery place. As long as it only affected her own work — or overwork — my mother-in-law fiercely resisted this attempt. Now, however, when it coincided with the interest of her own daughter, she opened wide the doors of the nursery to the persistent dispatcher's kid. The payoff was a lorry plus driver, reserved for us at the very moment the yards open and the nice warm bricks appear.

Life is a constant struggle. The battleground lies between the kiln and your lorry. Not a great distance, one might think. But the price difference is well known to the brickies too. Its distribution is the purpose of the struggle. The lorry is only allowed safe passage between the brickyard and your house, not a step nearer to the kiln. The first firing line is at the mouth of the kiln, the next one a running battle between kiln and lorry.

The grateful dispatcher told us which yard would have bricks on the day we wanted them. Without the information, we might have criss-crossed the whole county, from one brick factory to the next. The factories have to satisfy official orders first, among them deliveries to the building centre, and the fight concentrates on the small residue. We arrived there at the crack of dawn, only to find a crowd near the kilns, building centre tickets in their hands. With a ticket a brick only costs you about 4 forints. Getting the bricks on to the lorry costs 100 forints, or 150, maybe 200. The fight for bricks has no rules — if you want to stick to the rules, all you have to do is wait quietly at the centre until the bricks appear there, one by one. If, however, cheap bricks are more important than rules, you have to join battle. There's no point in working out a long-term strategy. The ranks of the enemy are constantly shifting. Guerilla tactics are best.

The clue to the battle lies in the brickies' contract, which does not oblige them to load the bricks on a private buyer's lorry. Nor does it appear on the ticket that one is entitled to the loading. On the other hand, the buyer's loaders aren't allowed to the loading bay. Brickies wear special asbestos gloves and can pick up the scorching hot brick while you cannot. They are thus in an excellent position from which to start negotiating with the vulnerable buyer. If they are tough enough, they can squeeze the buyer. Sometimes, they may overdo it, as in my case.

I became so indignant that I stormed into the office. They told me there that loading bricks was a loader's job. They were supposed to carry bricks from the kiln to the yard but no further. If they did carry them further, they could charge for the job. But not as much as 200 forints for a thousand bricks. The foreman took my side and punished the blackmailing team by directing them to an official delivery — they didn't get a single private customer the whole morning. We were directed to another kiln with the advice to use better tactics.

We withdrew to the lorry for a council of war with the driver; he knew the tactics better from experience. As in our ignorance we hadn't worked out any plan beforehand (like a line to the director of the brick factory which could have ensured instant delivery to our house), we turned to the driver to find out who was to be bribed. He was first in line, that was obvious. In exchange he led us to another foreman who pocketed 50 forints and directed us to another loading team. Their fee was only 100 forints for a thousand bricks. This money and the foreman's cut go no doubt into a common pool, to be redistributed later.

My team must have been one of pretty long standing. A brick factory is usually the first stop for those just freed from prison. The foremen spoke to their men like screws. The punishment meted out to my first team also showed they were utterly at the mercy of the foremen. After stitching paper bags in jail, earnings at the kilns are not too bad, but conditions of work are worse. In the course of my wanderings, I saw many brickyards, each ghastlier than the last. They differ only in their degree of primitiveness, meaning that the process between seller and buyer is handled exclusively by human labour. Without mechanical handling between kiln and lorry, morals and methods are those of the underworld.

My second team was hardly angelic. Once my lorry was loaded, I watched at my leisure how they tripped up the next customer. This character obviously thought of himself as an experienced operator. He must have been there before, as he made a beeline for the cheapest team. But he wanted to save himself the bribe to the foreman, and fell foul of the cunning brickies. His lorry was half loaded when they just sat down, saying they were too tired, they would carry on in the afternoon. He could either pay waiting time for his lorry, or raise the brickies' rate. He raised it. He'd wanted to save 50 forints off the foreman — and it cost him 400 to the brickies. For the money they screwed out of him, he could have bought the bricks at the building centre and had them delivered to his door, without losing a whole working day.

The battle at the brick factories is about very small sums of money. A few hundred forints from the buyer's pocket is just about the horizon of the brickies. They are fighting for really pitiful amounts but don't know any better. That's why they land in prison more often than not.

These petty criminals are, of course, well known to the police; once caught, their way to prison is easy and well-oiled. When they are released, their only way to survive is the brick factory. It's a sad statistic that most of them are gypsies.

It's a vicious circle. If they tried their luck at a less primitive brick factory, they would lose the premium on back-breaking labour. More modern factories take mostly semi-skilled workers to handle the machines. In the fullness of time, they may become trained operators at the conveyor belt, even team leaders. Provided they can read, write and are patient, they may advance to the status of skilled workers — at much lower immediate income. Then, and only then, can they join an established network that can ensure a more regular income on the side.

The return on this investment of time requires quite a lot of self-denial. Patience and a puritan life-style are plain luxury when you don't really know how long your freedom lasts. To have the vision to look beyond tomorrow; to refuse the first tart on offer after having feasted on pin-ups in your cell; not to pinch the bottle of vodka at the self-service; not to go to bed in a vacant villa; not to listen to pop music from the stolen transistor; — so to deny the pleasures of the flesh would require remarkable abstemiousness.

Finicky buyers can, of course, avoid confronting this underworld: they can go to the building centre. It's worth going there if you only need a few hundred bricks. In fact, it seems to be the social mission of a building centre to draw a veil before the eyes of sensitive buyers and protect them from the hellish depths beyond the brickyards.

In return for the driver's good advice, we presented him with our gloves. (The father of my tennis partner had brought a batch of industrial gloves from his workplace — 80 forints a pair in the shops.) The driver could keep them or sell them, — anyway, he was so satisfied that he booked only half a day's carriage to our account.

I suspect he sold the gloves to the government surplus stores — they buy anything and everything, with no questions asked. Working clothes, gloves, boots and so on have a prescribed period of usage — which must be awfully short. Once I went to buy overalls and saw a man dumping a sackful of practically new rawhide boots on the floor of the store: nobody asked how long they had been used.

We discovered another use for the building centre when cement and lime were needed. Surprisingly, sometimes they have something that's not available anywhere else, not even on the black market. Their price for cement is 60 forints per hundredweight. Private sector builder's merchants charge 70 — if they've got it. Unfortunately, the supply situation at the centre is rather uneven. Bricks are almost always available — most made in the outlying factories end up here. Cement, however, is in short supply across the country. Sometimes a couple of consignments arrive, only to be snapped up by those with prior bookings. Even if I were to spend all my days at the centre, there would be no guarantee that my number would come up. It would also be almost impossible to time the arrival of a 'black' lorry, the cement goes so fast. You have to make a split-second decision whether to rush to the office and order official delivery (during which time the cement may be taken away) or use the 'black' drivers who lurk around the centre at cement-time. They charge 20 forints for loading a sack, plus the fee for 'black' haulage.

My partner doesn't make snap decisions. I, for my part, hate lingering around the centre. We had to find another solution. This meant 100 forints to an office girl at the centre. She phoned my partner immediately cement arrived. My partner phoned my neighbour who already had a phone. The neighbour told me, I leapt in my car and rushed to my partner's office. Meanwhile, he had got hold of a company lorry. Together, we drove hell-bent to the centre and loaded the cement ourselves, saving the 20 forints per sack.

My partner's company, it so happened, was in the habit of offering the use of their lorries at cost price to its employees, to attract scarce staff. But only the lorries were on offer, drivers being scarcer than most. My partner was licensed to drive lorries; petrol coupons are provided in the usual manner, that is, twice the required amount. We sold the surplus petrol to a pump attendant who was known to us, thereby saving on the carriage.

The only trouble was my partner's peasant meanness. He worked out the quantity of petrol needed to the last drop, but forgot that our house stood on a hillside. On the steep slope, the residual fuel dribbled back from the engine into the tank and the lorry stalled, completely blocking the road. A bus had to stop behind us. More and more cars gathered behind it. Passengers swore cordially at us and we, to our eternal shame, had to beg some petrol by the cupful from aggrieved motorists. It was no joy to restart the lorry, with three tons of cement on it. And, on the way back, we had to re-purchase the petrol we'd sold — at a higher price.

This incident left a bad taste in my mouth. Anyway, there was renewed cement-trouble: our friend at the centre couldn't promise anything for weeks. Besides, my trust in my partner's driving skill had been shaken. It was then that I remembered P.

I had known P since childhood: he was the youngest son of the porter in the house where my mother lived. While I was still living there, I once pottered around with my car in front of the house. P came along and offered some unasked advice — good advice. It turned out that he was a passionate motorist and a passionate adviser. He was a skilled motor mechanic, working at a central car maintenance depot. I lost touch with him when I left my mother's house, but we became neighbours again when I moved to my father's flat. In the meantime he'd got married and moved in with his wife's family. The only difference between us was that I lived on a council estate — he lived in no-man's-land.

No-man's-land was a small area encircled by two branches of a new motorway, with two or three grotty houses on it. The place had no name either, only a number. By rights, his house had no reason to exist: according to the plans of the road-building Ministry of Transport, the area was to be purchased compulsorily and the inhabitants rehoused on a priority basis. By some strange coincidence, all the new housing available to the ministry was taken up by the engineers and workers who laboured devotedly on the new road. Therefore, the ministry graciously passed no-man's-land back to the local council.

What council housing there was fell to those at the head of the waiting list. No-man's-land remained free and independent, unwanted by either colonising power. The council admitted that P and his neighbours had every right to a new house — during the road-building, the area had become a rubbish dump and now the groggy walls were incessantly shaken by the heavy traffic on both sides — naturally, it was the job of the ministry to secure the housing.

The experts from the ministry accepted likewise that the inhabitants were fully entitled to new housing — their windows were at the height of the road-bed, three yards from the monster wheels of heavy lorries, the noise worse than at an airport; of course, it was the council's duty to allocate houses.

This curious warfare had been going on for several years. Nobody wanted a claim on no-man's-land. I called on P in this maelstrom, asking for his advice. He gave me more than that: he had cement and lime a-plenty. In exchange, I promised to find a way to get him a new home.

P had already written countless letters to the public complaint letterbox at the TV, with no result. The workings of this letterbox are twofold. The complaints department handles hundreds of thousands of letters, and passes on truly outrageous cases to the complaints programmers. Those will appear on the box, and pressure of public opinion ensures justice is done. That at least is the theory. In practice, you put pressure on the complaints department which, in turn, starts making inquiries of the offending authority, — hinting that they could be featured in a programme. Most of the time this is enough and the wrong righted.

I happened to have a schoolmate who worked at the TV. I handed him the file on P's case. My friend asked the head of complaints about P's original letters, as if on behalf of the programme department. The head had not been at fault: he does not have to deal with every single complaint, otherwise he would be smothered by them. Sometimes, however, he has to do something, otherwise the programme would lose its authority based on the touching public belief that it can settle grievances.

My friend offered him the chance to right a wrong, to uphold the prestige of his department and to safeguard the authority of his programme. P and his neighbours were rehoused. By the time our house came to be ready, — thanks, in large part, to P's supplies — P was also able to move to his new flat.

My relations with my partner may have cooled a little bit, but I found an understanding new partner in the person of P. Mutual gratitude is a very strong bond. I hardly ever had to ask him for something: his small van was always full of things I needed — lovely, crumbling cement (at 50 forints per hundredweight, including loading and carriage), lime at one third the going rate, and many other things. I gave him the key of the house, not only as a token of trust, but also so that he could offload whatever happened to turn up. There were many similar keys on his key-ring.

Once he turned up with a sack: did we want coathangers? Without waiting for a reply, he tossed down 200 coathangers — even today, I still wonder who to give them to. On no-man's-land, P had a constant store of desirable goods, but also kept subsidiary supplies in the garages of his beloved customers. He was the missing link between the demand of commerce and the supply of state resources.

P became an indispensable participant in the great game, a player of virtuosity, endowed with manifold talents. He made all the advantages of underhand procurement of both materials and moonlighters available. He more or less became an overseer, spotting our requirements weeks in advance, introducing new players whenever needed and watching with eagle eyes to ensure fair play. It was a virtuoso performance.

5. Double Dealers

Another player who appeared on the scene early on was Z. P, in his jeans, with his Afro hair-do, offered a sharp contrast to Z who wore a well-cut suit, knitted tie, carried an attaché case and, with his greying temples, looked rather like a diplomat. The only thing they had in common was a digital watch. Nevertheless, they complemented one another perfectly, at least as far as access to scarce supplies was concerned.

Z was good for timber at favourable prices; P's strong suit was cement, lime and the like. They had perfected artistic variations in the game of acquiring the requisite items, navigating the thickets of corruption and influence. I had no direct contact with P's employer. Our only link was his battered pick-up van. In Z's office I soon became a regular feature. I shared the coffee brewed by his secretary, and learned to judge the varying quality of the beverage at the beginning of each month and at the end of it; used Z's phone for business; listened and watched the devious means of supply management. The doorman smartly saluted me, as it behoved a valued customer.

Our first meeting with Z took place in the Narcissus espresso. My carpenter had by then prepared the drawings for the internal staircase, but I baulked at the stiff price he'd asked for building it. F and his mate were nearing the end of their work, and I wanted to get hold of the hardwood I needed. Not just any hardwood, but the particular quality specified by the carpenter. F took the order, but I wanted to have a look at it myself, so he had to introduce me to Z, his company's chief purchasing officer. The blinds in the Narcissus were still down when I met Z at 7 am, but the place was full of regulars from the neighbouring offices. The espresso was buzzing with hurried business deals. Z came straight to my table. I was obviously the only person there who wasn't a regular. He'd hardly downed his early morning brandy, and our deal was done.

He took me to the company's timber yard, where — for a bottle of wine — I was allowed not only to select my timber but also to have it cut to size. I thought I was going to have to settle with F, but Z discreetly handed me his visiting card, indicating that we could deal directly from then on. He also invited me to the sanctum of his office, in which I learned the finer points of backstage wheeling and dealing.

I gradually realised that without the network of backstage influences, the supply of goods and services between companies would be next to impossible. Only the uninitiated imagine that a company writes out a purchase order and, heigh-ho, the goods roll in from the supplier. This may happen, but not too frequently; old people sometimes whisper about such events in the good old days.

To make sure goods on order arrive in the right quantity and at the right time, managers have to use the network. Without personal contacts they wouldn't get very far. They have to do this, both for the advancement of individuals and for the broader interests of the company. The two are interlinked: it is in the interests of the company that only those people should move up the ladder who, through their personal contacts, can improve the efficiency of the firm; and efficiency (perhaps surprisingly) means prestige and goodwill.

Of course it goes without saying that everyone needs power, accumulated through useful acquaintances, just to safeguard their standing in the firm. Sometimes, however, this power cannot lead directly to a higher position, owing to one's job description. A secretary, for instance, may acquire quite a lot of power, through handling the boss's business deals; however, her advancement isn't as straightforward as that of her superior. The career of a junior manager can lead to progress up the higher grades: group leader, head of department, divisional director and so on, according to company hierarchy. The secretary's career stops at the manager director's anteroom, and sticks there — unless she decides to work for a public body, like the trade union, the Red Cross or something of the sort.

Therefore a secretary may accumulate quite a lot of potential power, while her boss must use up *his* potential in the network of mutual favours and obligations. This way, on occasion, a secretary may get hold of something in short supply sooner than her boss. Indeed, the boss himself may sometimes take advantage of his secretary's stock of influence. This is not a general rule, just a possibility.

These are all alternatives in the art of manipulating the network; this differs substantially from corruption, because it's not backhanders but mutual favours that make it work. This office network is not quite the same thing as the network of friends, schoolmates, neighbours and so on, though the two often overlap. It's a grey area, not black or white, and it's no good being dogmatic about clear-cut demarcations.

Both P and Z make use of the network, as well as of corruption, but they approach it differently. P enters the network at the end of the line, in getting supplies and transporting them. Z comes in at the start, in purchasing and procurement. Therefore P has very little pull in personal relations throughout the network (of course, he has some indirect pull through his own web of acquaintances and business partners), while Z has wide influence through a web of mutual favours and obligations. Corruption only plays a part in his game when it comes to actual deliveries. Therefore, P takes the greater risks and dangers as he has no protective network. Z, on the other hand, is protected by the web of mutuality.

Whenever I pass a building site, I usually ask the workers for a component, a tool or some hardware — they give it willingly. They have plenty of them, there's such a lot of loss and breakage that they don't notice it, so there's no risk involved for them. P's business is based on this fact of life. He, of course, works on the basis of 'planned loss'. His safeguard is money, greasing the appropriate palm. If need be, stock control can be falsified, the stores manager can cook the books, the driver's mate can make out phoney waybills. This, however, means a chain of risks. An overzealous inspector can affect the whole chain. Z, on the other hand, never handles the goods themselves.

His business is based on always ordering twice the quantity actually needed.

If one dismantled a housing estate built by a state enterprise, analysed its components and compared this 'demolition list' item by item with the materials originally requisitioned, delivered and utilised, the difference would be enough for another housing estate. Where did it all go? The surplus is absorbed by the house-building populace. One could account for every brick and plank. It's easy to check the figures — the number of houses approved by borough councils surpasses by far the quantities of materials needed for them, sold through the building centre and the trade. And this 'freely' available supply of building materials absorbs the surplus cash floating around, balancing supply and demand more efficiently than the commercial distribution system. Besides, it renders greater satisfaction all round.

Doubting Thomases could easily convince themselves of the superiority of our building technology: twice the number of houses built from the same quantity of materials, far surpassing the technology of richer, more advanced countries. Western concerns that use the most up-to-date technology would probably go bankrupt from such extravagance. Our enterprises are not as selfish and narrow-minded. Normally they could not match effective demand, as this would upset their yearly planning. Materials used are, of course, an element of costs, therefore part of GNP. So the enterprises strongly support the broad social policy of the state.

Z is therefore insured not by money, but by economic indices. The greater the nominal wastage of materials, the larger the company's contribution to the gross national product. Anyway, it's easier to get tripped up by money than by economic indices. Z's contribution to his company's planning and to the state's social policy enhances the protection given to him by the whole national economy. At a personal level, he is protected by his director, the director is protected by the ministry for industry, and so on.

The recognition of all this led me to two conclusions. Z is, of course, fully aware that half of all supplies ordered will disappear — so it's in his interest to have them disappear as near as possible to his level in the pecking order, and the only risk Z runs is the threat of scrutiny of the whole national economy. Not much of a threat when the thing works and the economy prospers in a socially useful way. Besides, Z can be quite confident, given the protection of the mutual-interest network, that even if such scrutiny did take place, the retribution would start at P's level, not his.

Corruption and the mutual-interest network, however, do not only differ according to the measure of risk involved. There is also a qualitative leap between the activities of P and Z. Just as — according to Marx — new social relationships emerge in the framework of an old system, corruption is the parent of the mutual-interest network. This phenomenon, being two aspects — form and content — of the same development, lends itself to an analysis by marxist dialectics. From a technical point of view, the two stages resemble the relationship of guilds to early manufacture, or that of manufacture to mass production. Corruption has no complex intermediary stages. It is almost as simple as direct barter. It's a form of give-and-take, linking a quantifiable number of articles to a measurable number of people. When it so happens that the article drops out of normal trade circulation — or never appears in it — its scarcity means the buyer has to pay a premium for the privilege of acquisition.

The mutual network enfolds this simple truth in a sucession of shimmering veils. The precondition for new relationships is a bureaucratic apparatus, which in time will enmesh the whole of industry and spread its tentacles into commerce and services as well. Eventually, it unifies the three spheres, spreading its own official peculiarities into economic life and absorbing economic methods into public affairs and government. It constitutes its own economic system of give-and-take, run according to certain rules of social etiquette. An outside observer would only see the choreography: friendly conversation, polished manners, courteous behaviour. In fact, these are not mere formalities, but the essence. Without them, one may give but will not take. Money is a superficial factor here, often a quite negligible one.

In contrast to the direct barter of corruption, this is truly an essential, qualitative transformation. There is no better proof of this qualitative difference than the fact that the network is actually taxed. Those who buy their cars not through the state agency but through a particular institution, claiming from its special allocation, have to pay 10 per cent more — the price of jumping the queue. Within the relationships of the network it is not measurable units of goods that change hands between identifiable persons. The system of mutual favours must operate even when no goods are available — or, indeed, needed — as relationships have to be nurtured regardless. This represents a higher level of culture, compared to which direct barter is barbarous.

The network can be regarded as a long-term credit system, pre-supposing the possession of collaterals — just as primitive exchange cannot exist without a willing buyer with cash in hand.

It is interesting to note that the dialectical leap from lower to higher forms also has a special effect: the higher will influence the lower.

"I should be very grateful... ", I say to the shop assistant. I can't just say: "Here's a hundred."

Thus the more elevated behaviour influences the most primitive corruption, though, within the mutual-interest network, money will seldom be mentioned.

All this may be a universal feature of development; however, one also has to keep an eye on local conditions. In our country, more as well as less developed relationships exist peacefully side by side, thoroughly intermingled. Bribery alone would limit one's opportunities, using only the network likewise. One has to play the game at both levels.

It wasn't my concern for other players in my team that led me to analyse the different strands of the network, or the risks involved in either this or in outright corruption, let alone pure theoretical interest. All I wanted to find out was the ideal approach to securing supplies. As a result, I know now that the ideal way (as usual) is the middle way: use the system of mutual favours and obligations to get hold of permits and other paperwork, while being prepared where appropriate to slip a few banknotes into a greasy palm.

There is no shortage of Hungarocell insulating blocks. They're available at the building centre, at 1,100 forints per cubic metre. However, as the insulation of the roof and walls required 10 cubic metres — 11,000 forints worth not including delivery — it did not seem sensible to buy. I remembered seeing lots of broken Hungarocell blocks in my skiing partner's garage. He is a scientist, and got them from the company that packed his factory's export consignments. Sometimes he had to check the packing of delicate instrumentation, and was on good terms with a manager at the packing company. Sometimes he was presented with a load of Hungarocell offcuts, which he then passed on to a sculptor friend. It's of course in the interest of the packers that complex instruments should arrive safely — they would have to pay for broken units.

My friend introduced me to this manager who — over and above a cordial reception — also disclosed to me that his company allowed its employees (and their friends and acquaintances) to buy up broken Hungarocell blocks at 150 forints per cubic metre, roughly one seventh of building centre prices. All I had to do, he said, was to go to their main depot and contact a certain storekeeper who would know what offcuts were available that day.

I drove out to the depot, found the storekeeper, who knew I was coming — and emphasised to him my deep conviction of the importance of the role he was playing. As proof of my reverence I slipped him 100 forints, whereupon he explained that in his opinion, asking 150 forints for the offcuts was daylight robbery — they were second-class rubbish, not worth more than 90 forints. He had only about one cubic metre in stock, he said, but told me to go back to head office, pay for one cubic metre of second-class Hungarocell at 90 forints, then come back with the receipt and a hired van. I'd better hurry, he said, to get to the office before lunchtime.

I thanked him for the good advice, hinting that my regard would be unceasing in future too, rushed back and caught the cashier in good time, flagged down a 'black' driver and returned to the store. After handing over a further 200 forints, I wasn't too surprised to find my lorry loaded with 10 cubic metres of first-class Hungarocell in perfect condition. They scattered some broken pieces on top, useful bonus to make my friend's sculptor friend happy. The whole transaction cost me 500 forints — one twentieth of the official price which didn't include delivery.

Cutting the price of Hungarocell had required coordination

between four people. It was a clear example of the link between the network and corruption. First, between my skiing partner and myself, there was pure friendship. Second, between him and the packing manager, an official contact. Third, the link between the manager and the storekeeper was the superior-subordinate pattern, finally enhanced by corruption. Without greasing the palm of the storekeeper, I would have got nowhere: one cubic metre of offcuts was good for nothing. Even with knowledge of the firm's internal customs, however, corruption alone couldn't have done the trick: without the help of the manager I could not have got a waybill, without the receipted invoice, the storekeeper couldn't have given me any offcuts at all. All of which goes to show that one has to have a strong sense of discrimination as to where the different approaches mesh.

The best way to interlock the two approaches of the mutual network and of corruption is to adjust the pressure of administrative linkages from above to the demands of corruption from below. I learnt the lesson at the brick factory: the minimum of bribery had to be calculated from the bottom up. My trouble in that particular case was that pressure from above was missing.

The manner in which I procured our heating oil tanks approached the ideal even closer: in this instance, the roles played by manager and storekeeper were performed by one and the same person: consequently it was pure network and no corruption.

At Ferroglobus, the state supply company, a new oil tank of 6 cubic metres costs 32,000 forints. This was the size required by the blueprints and by fire regulations. The price was light years beyond our means. We browsed in vain for quite a while in the small ad columns, hoping some company might scrap a tank somewhere. Eventually it was the constant nagging of relatives, friends and acquaintances that brought forth a valuable piece of news: not far from the capital, a chemical factory was going to be dismantled.

This factory had been built under a West German licence; not only the technology and the machinery were imported, but everything else, down to the last nut and bolt. The only thing that was not imported was skilled labour, for putting up the factory. Outwardly, the factory looked spick and span, as if a crane had lifted it from the Rhineland and had put it down next to the Danube, all glass and aluminium. Their confidence was, alas, somewhat misplaced. On the day the plant was completed, the feeder trolleys seized up inside the furnaces. They'd built the workshops with a measure of nonchalance; the machinery was out of alignment by a mere hair's breadth but that was enough to wreck the entire plant.

Now they were trying to recover what they could. A few billion marks had gone down the drain, perhaps a few million forints could still be salvaged from the ruins. The machinery was sold off piecemeal to other plants, steel scrap was shipped off to be melted down, the rest flogged to all-comers.

We hoped it would be an Aladdin's cave and rushed out to the scene. We made contact with the chief engineer of the demolition contractors. The site was a marvel to behold. Unfortunately, the stuff was much too good for our purposes. Everything was monster-sized. We could have bought any of the huge storage tanks for a pittance, but that would have left no room for the house on our plot. My partner was so carried away by the prospect of such a bargain that he suggested we should buy an extension to our plot and put the tank there. I had to point out to him that no amount of bribery would persuade the fire safety officers to pass such an enormous unit.

We were back to square one, all our contacts exhausted. However, the sight of incredible wastage at the demolition site recalled, somewhat ironically, the slogan of my pioneer days: 'Save metal, save paper!' and this began a chain of reminiscences from the depth of childhood, of the time when I'd collected not only metal and paper (for the national economy) but also matchbox labels (for myself). Curiously enough, my father had also joined in my collecting passion and, with his broader horizons, found out there was a collectors' club which he joined on my behalf. Many a Sunday was spent happily swopping labels with other members; there was one among them who regularly presented me, and other youngsters, with the well-known 'Save metal!' label, in many colours. Thanks to him, I had a complete set.

Now, I thought, if he'd had such an inexhaustible supply of these labels, he must have worked for the state scrap processing bureau. What if I looked him up? I wrote to my father who, luckily, remembered the name and address of the man. I called on him on the pretext of wanting to sell my collection of match-box labels, a complete set covering 20 years — would there be a market for it?

It seemed that my youthful enthusiasm — soaking boxes, drying labels on blotting paper, raiding my friends' attics for old boxes — had not been in vain. My collection was worth quite a tidy sum, my old mentor told me — still, far from enough to pay for a brand new oil tank. He'd moved since from the scrap agency to a steel stockist, but his new firm also dealt in second-hand goods, he said, and for old times' sake he was willing to help me with my oil tank problems which I'd mentioned to him in passing.

He promised to try and sell my collection at the club. He also asked all his yard managers throughout the country to report to him the arrival of any second-hand oil tank. His position in the firm was strong enough to compel the managers to do this, regardless of whether someone local had already paid them for reserving the tank.

Following one or two false starts, he phoned me to say that two 3,000-litre aluminium tanks had arrived at a nearby yard, at 6,000 forints. Beautiful, rustproof, everlasting units, way beyond my wildest dreams. He proposed we should go down together next weekend.

The story of the aluminium tanks, as he related it on the way, was quite interesting. The agronomist of a neighbouring vineyard wanted the tanks for himself and had contrived that they should be scrapped. However, a nationalised estate can only do this through a nationalised second-hand dealer; the idea was that the agronomist would then purchase from the second-hand outfit. However, he'd made a fatal error. The two tanks (in mint condition) were duly scrapped and sold to the second-hand yard. But when the agronomist arrived, he was in for a shock. The price of aluminium items, fixed by state decree, was so high that he simply couldn't afford the tanks.

When we confronted the price tag, our shock was only a shade less than that of the agronomist. The tanks cost 6,000 forints *each*. I'd been confidently budgeting for 6,000 all told.

Luckily, my old friend the label collector hadn't lost his paternal feelings towards me. Seeing the evident disappointment on my face, he took the local manager to one side and said something to him. Whereupon the manager asked me to come to the office. An invoice was handed to me — for four hundred-weights of aluminium scrap — at 1,500 forints the hundredweight. In fact, the two tanks weighed eight hundredweights. In Budapest, I smartly paid 6,000 forints at the firm's headquarters. Within a week, an articulated lorry delivered the two tanks.

My old friend did not disclose to me the secrets of their bookkeeping. It was obvious he had given me a present, much as he'd given me matchbox labels. Pulling rank, he must have asked the manager for a favour, no doubt about that. The weighbridge at the yard has a capacity of 40 tons; a hundredweight error was neither here nor there. The important thing was that the manager had the protection of the office network, and couldn't come to harm for his unselfish gesture.

To come by the two tanks in this manner was bordering on the miraculous. We could hardly expect another when we came to the radiators. Our warm family home came about almost in spite of string-pulling or corruption. It was more than a miracle — it was luck.

Our set of steel frame radiators stands as a work of art, celebrating the triumph of socialist consumer society. It is the exception reinforcing the rule — the general rule of network plus corruption.

Steel radiators are in such short supply that a sizeable minority of house-builders had conceded defeat, heating their houses in whatever primitive manner they could. For instance, I have a friend, a peace-loving character, who retired almost completely from the murderous battle for a solid home: he lives in a wooden shack throughout the year and, instead of heating, gets inner warmth from the marijuana growing on the flat roof of his shed. Noticing my progressive de-humanisation through my struggle for steel radiators, he took me to a commune.

Its members were united against the emotional impoverishment of civilisation. There is nothing unusual in this. What distinguished them from similar ventures was their refusal of all the means and measures applied by members of the consumer society for their comfort or advantage. They didn't try to find useful contacts, they didn't offer bribes to shop assistants, they didn't use 'black' drivers or moonlighters.

They worked out the quantities of materials needed for a house: cement, lime, sand, bricks and so on, placed orders for these at the building centre, waited until everything arrived, then got down to building their house. They used only basic raw materials — so much so that they cast their radiators from concrete!

They connected water pipes throughout the house in a labyrinthine manner, cast concrete over them, and that was that. Hot water runs through the pipes and heats up the concrete, it's as simple as that. They created different shapes in every room, painting the conduits different colours — it was a permanent pop art exhibition, that house. If anything went wrong in the conduit, they simply cast another piece, for next to nothing.

Even their old tank was cast from concrete, to which they applied three coats of varnish. For six years, not a drop of oil had seeped out.

The members of the commune lived and worked like the pioneering settlers of the new world, using only their own tools, clearing the wilderness for a better future. They regarded with contempt not only the degenerate descendants of early America, today's industrial society, but our more highly developed system too (even though ours creates a more intimate relationship between labour and its reward). In their view, one must keep clear of an economy based deliberately on the existence of shortages. They reckoned they might not be strong enough to change the system, but were certainly brawny enough to build in concrete — a permanent (and ironic) memorial to the economy based on 'planned shortages'. They translated pop art — an excrescence of western over-consumption — into Hungarian; they cast into concrete the symbol of our craving for the 'good life': Permanent Shortage. In this, they have been faithful to socialist realism in art. In contrast to their school, our heating system is almost a spiritual achievement, a standing retort to socialist commerce.

I was impressed by the concrete casting but not by the philosophy. My encounter with the commune did not tempt me to a radical break with society, however attractive this may have looked at the time; utopian thinking of this kind is alien to my nature. I couldn't countenance conversion to concrete architecture in my home, however desperate the prospects for the genuine article. I put my trust in society, that is, in my belief in the network and in corruption.

But what was the use of my philosophy, my principles firmly grounded in experience, if I had no radiators? Steel frame radiators are manufactured in one place only in the whole country, at the steel works in Dunaújváros. They are made on one set of single-purpose machinery, in limited batches. For two months, they turn out only one size of radiators, then they reset the machines and make a different size for another two months, and finally the third size for the next two months. There are only three standard sizes, so if someone misses a particular batch (as we did), they have to wait for six months until the manufacturing and trading cycle starts again.

The heating engineer had warned us about this timetable in summer, but by then it was too late. It looked as if we would have to postpone moving in until the spring, as we didn't fancy an unheated house. Without the radiators, the beautiful new tanks would be of no use. The production cycle of the radiators was an unshakable fact, as rigid as a law of physics. No amount of string-pulling or corruption could have stopped the machines and re-set them.

My partner considered the case so hopeless that, when he came across a set of cast iron radiators, he bought them at double the price, in full knowledge of their short life expectancy. Admittedly, he was in a tight corner, as he had to surrender his old cottage not later than December. Besides, he had become increasingly suspicious of me, thinking that I'd got addicted to dabbling in concrete, driven to utopianism by my despair. Whenever he spotted me in the neighbourhood of the cement mixer he became jumpy.

He was also unsure of my conversion to the value system of socialist consumerism and probably thought I might relapse into a philosophical refusal of the entire system. The cast iron radiators were *his* insurance that he would remain immune to infection by 'infantile disorder' of communalism.

I didn't take his suspicions amiss, but I wasn't prepared to accept defeat in the same way. Nor was I willing to succumb to the esoteric ideas of the commune. Remaining faithful to my principles, however, didn't bring the radiator-problem any nearer to solution. Our whole strategy had been based on the assumption that by the beginning of winter we would be able to move in. My partner was succumbing to defeatism. I had to embark on an outflanking action, to shake off creeping dejection. I left the capital, spurred on by a piece of advice picked up from somewhere that perhaps there was a godforsaken corner of the country where the radiator-allocation had been late arriving.

The steel works behind me, I set out against the current for the provinces. My spirits were raised by the news in one muddy village after another: yes, they had some No. 900 radiators some time ago. The farther out I went, the later the date.

I promised palpable proof of my gratitude to various shopkeepers, so there was no lack of good advice. In a small market town, a shopkeeper suggested that I should nip over to Kosd, a village I'd never heard of before. There was a hardware store there. However, when I got there, I found only a general store. In my disappointment, I bought a drink to wash down my chagrin and, in passing, idly asked the cashier whether she'd seen any radiators. She directed me to the store manager, a grumpy middle-aged person. I told him my sob-story, whereupon he asked me:

"Are you from a public body?"

"No, I'm a private buyer," I replied, losing what little hope I had.

"In that case," he said, "you can have radiators, No. 900. How many?"

For the first time in my life I started to stammer. I told him the quantity, uttering the words with some difficulty.

"OK," he said, "go to the yard at the end of the road, they'll make out the advice note, then come back here to pay."

I rushed to the yard in the outskirts and found the storekeeper at lunch. The yard was full of wheelbarrows, spades, rakes, trolleys, all the usual stuff of a hardware store — but no radiators. All the radiators had been taken away by the local co-operative, said the storekeeper with great regret. I tried waving the magic banknote before his eyes — it was of no use. His greedy eyes were proof he had none left. My frustration was complete: I could see the imprint the radiators had left in the ground. Perhaps he could get some back from the co-op? No hope, he said, with tears in his eyes.

I went back to the store manager and complained bitterly. He listened without a word. Once I finished, he picked up the phone and called the storekeeper. The poor man got the dressing down of his life; the manager's voice was trembling with fury.

"Haven't I told you to reserve 20 per cent of every consignment for private buyers?" he shouted down the line. "I turn my back for one single day, and you mess it all up! I've given strict instructions, god only knows how many times, that no public body is allowed to buy more than 80 per cent of anything," he turned to me apologetically. The sales assistants around him were suitably impressed. I wasn't, even though he asked for my address and phone number and promised that come hell or high water, he'd get the radiators for me soon.

Next morning the phone rang at 7 a.m.: Kosd was on the line. It was the store manager: "Come and collect the radiators."

I wasn't sure if I was still dreaming when I saw the set of radiators standing to attention in the forecourt. I paid 3,200 forints and loaded the treasure on my van. The store manager helped me carry them, his manner gruff and taciturn as before. I tried in vain to mollify him. I felt somehow embarrassed to slip him the envelope with the token of my gratitude. It was no good: he firmly waved aside all my approaches, giving me to understand that such gestures were out of place. He knew as well as I did that when a sales assistant shows great cordiality, they expect a bribe. His pretended bad manners were the sign of his refusal; in order to safeguard his personal honesty, he assumed the mask of a rude shopkeeper. Had he tried to couple his honesty with friendliness, my confusion would have been complete, his likely and inevitable moral rebuke too embarrassing. He had no intention to rebuke me, so he assumed the mantle of unfriendliness.

How could I pay homage to this amazing honesty? I asked for the complaints book and, in contrast to the coarse comments and rude remarks assembled there, I penned a hymn of effusive praise to the store's thoughtful care for the private customer, according to the best traditions of honest shopkeepers.

When it came to finding the missing link between oil tank and radiators, that is the boiler, we had to resort to the customary methods of acquisition. Of course, one cannot just walk in to the one and only store stocking boilers and walk out with a boiler under one's arm. Steel frame radiators are in short supply because of the rigid production programme, but there is no rhyme and reason in the making of boilers. Sometimes one can get imported boilers whereas there is no import licence for radiators. The director in charge of boiler sales (a patient of my wife's dentist uncle) said that he could get us a local make of boiler, suitable for burning both oil and solid fuel. We did appreciate the foresight of the designer of this, in view of the impending energy shortage, and appreciated even more that the benevolent influence of the director allowed us to dispense with bribery and corruption. Within a month, the boiler was ours, at 9,000 forints official price and no extras.

The next problem was a suitable oil burner to fit the boiler. Well-informed sources acquainted with the short-comings of the home-made kind advised us to try and get an imported unit. I wrote to my father about it, but — even through the syndicate — it would have been far more expensive than the Hungarian equivalent.

Before settling the question I decided to visit the company selling oil burners. At reception, the exotic plants sweating in tropical heat were an eloquent testimony to the efficiency of their products. The salesman explained the advantages and drawbacks of imported burners in an engaging manner, emphasising the merits of their after-sales service. He also pointed out the latest Hungarian-made burner, a carbon copy of the Western unit. We bought it for 14,000 forints. When we dismantled it at home, we found that it was not only copied but pirated — more than half the components had been made abroad. This might have explained why it was so cheap. They probably used the foreign components to establish the reputation of the new product on the market; or maybe they just bought up a lot of components at wholesale prices, assembled them with local labour and marketed them under the label: 'Made in Hungary'.

We felt justified pride at the success of socialist industry, at the dexterity of our export-import agencies in finessing the oil crisis, at the public-spiritedness of internal trade organs. As behoves good patriots, we spread the fame of the new burner and also gave proof of our internationalism, by praising the foreign components, as well as the quality of Hungarian workmanship shown in skilful assembly.

The success of the oil burner was so overwhelming that they stopped production of it. When they resumed production a year later and put the price up 5,000 forints, enthusiastic buyers paid over the odds to get a new one, by slipping an extra 3,000 forints to the sales assistant. They ended up with a home-made burner as expensive as an imported one and still made everybody happy.

The mutual network extends its protection in cases of this nature too. Corruption, in this instance, defeats its object: the unwary buyer slips 3,000 to the sales assistant, believing they have pulled a fast one on the commercial system. On the contrary: it's industry and trade that gain in the end. The buyer will pay for the shortfall created by those who, having contacted the secretary, the manager, the commercial director through their friends, claim scarce goods. Satisfying this hidden demand is, in effect, an advantage to the company; one official will scratch the back of another, enabling the firm to complete its annual plan.

In addition to the official interest, there is also a private interest. The company official, by means of bestowing a favour, places an obligation on someone else, to be encashed now or later. If they have no need for it, a relative, friend or neighbour can cash the blank cheque. In addition, when they ask for a corresponding favour on behalf of someone else they don't exhaust the fund of obligations, having only signalled goodwill. Both sides remain linked. By obtaining scarce goods for one another, officials of different enterprises will build up increasingly close bonds with managers on the other side; links of friendship will be inbred with the spirit of the network.

There is no danger of alienation, isolation or bureaucratic depersonalisation ever occurring, as long as there is scarcity of goods. The mutual network encompasses everyone in the know. In the system of favours and obligations, money plays an insignificant role; there is no loss of profit to the firm, as the mutual favours lead to considerable savings. There is no loss on faulty goods either — these are flogged to those who come into the shop off the street.

The real loser in this hidden commerce is the shop assistant — their potential under-the-counter income is shared out among the insiders before the goods reach the shop. This gives rise to the curious fact that in the case of goods not in commercial retail circulation (like bricks) bribery at the end of the line is minimal.

In commerce and trade the last in line, the shop assistant, has to demand a hefty cut. The naive buyer has to pay for missing out on familiarity with the network, and also to pay a premium for the higher risk the shop assistant is taking. That poor soul is not protected by the invisible safeguards of the network.

6. Plain Dealers

'We have seriously considered the proposal that a notice should be conspicuously displayed in our shops saying that tips or secret payments are strictly forbidden. After long discussion, we have come to the conclusion that a notice of this nature would not solve the problem', — wrote the director of the State Clothing Chainstore in a popular periodical. The discussion was indeed long and arduous at the mass meeting of commercial employees. Isn't it a touching sign of internal democracy that the bosses didn't argue about a matter of great public interest behind closed doors?

Anyway, good sense carried the day. For shop assistants, this was no joke. They tend to knock off at 6 p.m. as a rule, and if they want to spend some time in the bosom of their family, they cannot take on a second job to earn the extra income conducive to family harmony unless they are prepared for remonstrations and sarcastic comments about smarter relatives or neighbours. The shop assistant is just as much in favour of peaceful family life as the buyer who, having called at the shop in vain during the day, is reluctant to be exposed to examples of others' success in acquiring some scarce article.

The shop assistant must, therefore, gain this wherewithal at the work place, unlike the others who can do this off the job. Some stores were actually toying with the idea of applying the ultimate sanction: dismissal for repeated offences. Luckily, good sense was victorious here too, perhaps not so much because of the menacing stance adopted by the shop assitants, more as a result of the scarcity of labour. As the director quoted above wrote: 'In view of the perpetual labour shortage, our stores are increasingly compelled to adopt a complete self-service system. However, while this has its positive aspects, it does not offer a perfect solution, in as much as many purchasers continue to demand the attendance of a shop assistant.' With good reason...

The said director, having discarded the idea of sanctions as impractical, turned to scientific analysis for a solution. His findings — historical and anthropological — are perhaps not too surprising: 'The phenomenon of extra payments to staff by buyers was first encountered in our chain about 20 years ago, especially in the men's-wear departments.' This statement, indicating a long history of male chauvinism, is followed by the acute observation: 'We know that the act of passing money underhand is occurring in a fairly sophisticated manner (whispered conversation, cordial handshake in the fitting room, ushering the buyer to the door) and the shop assistants are very circumspect in avoiding the presence of any witness to the act. This may be one reason why complaints from customers are of rare occurrence.'

The author then proceeds to set up a typology of the ways and means of this exchange, breaking new ground in economic sociology:

'The customer is properly served and he slips the money to the assistant of his own volition;

'The shop assistant is ostentatiously helpful and drops a hint that this should be rewarded;

'The assistant demands the money in a skilfully provocative manner;

'The customer makes an offer before stating his requirements.'

The truth of these is beyond doubt. We should be grateful to the marketing researchers and their clients for devoting their precious time to science, instead of using it to make sales under the counter: their contribution is more valuable than the discussion, in general terms, of 'the secondary economy' by academic economists in more serious theoretical journals. One of these scientists made the informed guess that out of a total yearly income of the whole population, reckoned at 300 billion forints, at least 10 billion goes on bribery, for which he coined the delightful euphemism 'thanksgiving money'.

This scientific worker may have spent some of his mental

capital on his treatise without being involved in any sacrifice. The devoted shop assistant, who supplied data for the director, probably had to forego some 'thanksgiving money'. The fact that data collection may postpone — or indeed eliminate — the threat of disciplinary action is poor consolation for the loss.

The director, cashing an intangible 'letter of credit' (a felicitous term used by another sociologist) gained through the mutual network, draws on an asset worth infinitely more than the 10 billions of 'thanksgiving money'. The difference in value could, however, only be established if the powers that be would pursue an audit in the 'solidarity bank' of network members and would attempt to put a price tag on goods and services distributed through the channels of mutual favours and obligations, such as trading licences, tax concessions, personal promotions, exemptions obtained through patronage. The auditor may find that, in consequence, those most suited or best qualified don't get appropriate jobs, or that better quality goods hardly ever get distributed. Our sociologist friend calls this process 'the chain of counter-selective decisions'; the auditor, in his closing report, may find that even those on the inside track will suffer from the system in the long run, — albeit in a descending order. The director suffers less than the shop assistant, who is less affected than the customer, who has to pay 'thanksgiving money'.

Let us assume the director sets aside a pair of coveted jeans for a friend, the borough councillor; in exchange, the director's nephew is awarded a plumber's trade licence. If a tap is dripping in the shop assistant's — or customer's — kitchen, and the plumber makes a botched job of it (seeing they couldn't get a licence on the strength of skill and training), the price for the counter-selective decision will have to be paid through constant repair bills.

On the other hand, it may be that the plumber is perfectly capable of a solid job, but the plumber's uncle, the director, forgot to exchange the plumber's 'letter of credit' for an imported water-tap, available only in special shops. That would require another pair of Levi's. The shop assistant is in no position to ask the customer for a trade licence, nor can the customer offer such a thing in exchange. If they want a pair of Levi's, they have to pay. To cover the next plumber's bill, and the one after that, more and more jeans must disappear under the counter. If the wretched shop assistant wants a drip-proof tap, they must appear in the guise of a customer at the kitchenware store. So it comes to pass that the sales assistant will have to save up on jeans to palm-grease required for the tap, while the clerk at the kitchenware store has to cheat customers for the sake of the precious jeans.

There may be an intermediate variant to this equation. Take the case of the provincial plumber who can't find enough moonlighting, and whose application for a 'private sector' trade licence is always refused since the quota is exhausted by granting licences through patronage. The plumber too wants a pair of Levi's, and can only get them by paying for them out of a hard-earned salary. Odd jobs (mostly from friends and relatives) are just about enough to pad out the housekeeping money and no more. The plumber would have to change jobs to gain the advantages the shop assistant enjoys — not always easy.

The plumber could never hope to aspire to the advantages of directors, who, together with other shareholders of the 'solidarity bank', belong to an exclusive circle where ordinary mortals are not allowed. Club membership is for ever, lost only by making a really big mistake.

'Letters of credit' carry a higher rate of interest than money. Directors can manipulate the stock of jeans in various ways. By thoughtful distribution throughout the network, they can build up new credits. By placing orders for smaller quantities than the volume of demand, they can maintain a fund of more or less stable value, without risking the outcry too glaring a shortage would provoke. The shop assistant is hemmed in by the actual amount of stock ordered by the boss — the director is in charge of supply and demand.

Of course, operating the network is only a secondary activity for the director, whose main concern is the profitability of the company. If there is a good profit, the director's is several times greater than the sales assistant's bonus. The profitability of the firm depends not on the internal distribution of scarce goods, but on customers coming in search of such scarce items and, not finding them, reluctantly accepting the second-rate. So the director can boost income through the available goods rendering the profit, and increase 'credit' by manipulating scarce articles. The poor shop assistant is restricted to under-the-counter activities on scarce items — palms don't get greased for freely available goods. All the shop assistant can hope for is a small bonus at the end of the day. The director, by artificially maintaining some scarcity, can enhance the value of a 'shareholding' and, at the same time, customers cannot grumble that nothing is there to be had.

Therefore, a shop is a place where you can either get something or you can't. It sounds a paradox. Whenever you go shopping in the ordinary way, you can't get anything you want. If I personally tried to get walnut veneer, resin or white spirit for the cabinetmaker; a contact breaker, conduit or fusebox for the electrician; cement for the bricklayer; tiles or clamps for the slater and so on, I wouldn't be able to. Yet, when I look at the house, what do I see? The bricklayers built the wall, with cement in it. The electrician fixed the conduit, fitted the contact breaker to the fusebox. Everything necessary materialised.

Zeno, the father of dialectics, would not need to worry about finding paradoxes today: they exist in abundance. He would be hard put to it, indeed, to find situations which are not paradoxical. The theory of accumulation which is derived from Zeno's dialectics, has its counterpart in my theory of 'permanent shortage'. This theory prevented me from succumbing to the attractions of the 'philosophy of concrete' pursued by the commune, and, at the same time, helped me to acquire what existed or did not exist (as the case may be). The truth is one, but divisible. I grew up on dialectics and I owe a debt of gratitude to its inventor, Zeno, that I have been able to find my way through the paradoxes of contradictory true statements, as laid down by the law of dialectics. Unlike so many of my contemporaries who were unable to make use of the doctrine, I have not lost my faith in dialectical materialism. Scarce goods can be conceived of as 'a moving body' which 'neither moves where it is in existence, nor is at rest where it is in existence'. The truth is that they are scarce but divisible, albeit divisible only selectively. The key term is: selective distribution.

This can be pursued in many ways. The capitalist way is rationing by the purse — prices perform the selection among purchasers. Such reification is, however, unworthy of our socialist system, in its current stage of development. In the previous stage, while we were merely laying the foundations of socialism, the decisive human factors of selective distribution were patience and perseverance. There would be endless queues snaking in front of the shops. Today, the queues have largely disappeared, having been replaced by 'circular entities' emanating from the back door of the shop instead of the front entrance.

In the outdoor markets one does sometimes see a genuine black marketeer, surrounded by a ring of eager customers; there may also be constant movement between shops, but primitive queues have been done away with.

Having laid down the foundations, quantitative indices have been replaced by qualitative ones, in perfect harmony with the law of dialectics. Patience (commendable, perhaps, in those who are still expecting the fulfilment of pure communism) has ceased to be a selective factor and has been replaced by rationality (in those, who having reached the uppermost stage of socialism, prefer to lay the groundwork for their houses, rather than for the system).

In the past, those who persevered hardest in the queue gained a rather meagre recompense: today, the lushest rewards go to those who find a way to bypass the queue. It's not enough to know how to read between the lines — one has to squeeze through them.

One must understand that the material powers of the state have their limits. It would be unreasonable to expect every single article to be available at every shop. Indeed, it is highly commendable that the state has transcended the crude capitalistic principles of the cash-nexus. It has also risen way above the erstwhile arbitrary centralised distribution that gave so much offence to the expectant population. 'Man is the supreme value', we are wont to say, so why not entrust him with selective distribution?

Is the state's economic power less than omnipresent? Selective distribution of scarce goods becomes a highly respected social task. People willingly share the burdens of the state and undertake the delicate task of distribution. They complement the shortcomings of the state by their own surplus of rationality. In our more advanced type of society, human qualities are worth more than mere objects, humanity achieves its due dignity, rising above the obsolete universe of relations between objects.

The grand five-year plan, laid down by the state, does not

say who should get what and who shouldn't. Therefore people are allowed to follow personal plans. Brains democratically gain appropriate social recognition, talents get their due reward. Long queues were dispersed not by brute force or prohibition: we, the rational people, put an end to them. Rational co-operation between shop assistant and customer put paid to the crude constraint of queuing.

This is real self-service. The director may have stumbled on some basic truths when he wrote: 'Many buyers do demand the attendance of a shop assistant' and 'complaints are of rare occurence' — but I don't think he perceived the strength of the spiritual bond between shop assistant and purchaser. We have to admit, of course, that there are still shortcomings in this field. There are a few conservative shopworkers as well as old-fashioned customers who have yet to recognize the wide social horizons unfolding before their eyes. It may be true that 'social existence determines consciousness', — as Marx said — but some remnants of the past do linger on. The new foundations have been well and truly laid; the superstructure is still not complete.

This relationship between shop assistant and customer has a special feature, distinguishing it from the dealings of those who enter via the network, namely a reverence for talent. The ablest and best qualified are not winnowed out here. Life may be easier in the exclusive circles frequented by the director — but what's the use of earthly goods, without the spiritual rewards of nobler human character-traits? The director, it could be argued, is deprived of the simple wisdom of ordinary people.

In the interplay of shop assistant and customer, it is the un-talented who will be winnowed out. This is an open contest; prerogatives, influence, social origin do not count. If one cannot get hold of whatever it is one wants, one can only blame oneself. In the olden days, everybody put the blame for the shortages on the system — rightly too, when ten units were put in the shop-window, and a thousand people watched them disappear. Since we have abolished queues, such deplorable spectacles cannot occur any more. If there is nothing in the shopwindow — except, perhaps, a rare specimen for show purposes only, 'not for sale' — it will depend on the alertness and ingenuity of the customer to find the hidden article. The age of what Georg Lukacs called

The Destruction of Reason is over. Our system devolves on its citizens not only the house-building programme, but the responsibility for failure too: if you are not alert enough to be able to put up your house, blame your own grey matter, not the system.

The theory of 'permanent shortage' enables one — at the very beginning of a shopping expedition — to dispense with that part of the truth which might suggest that the situation is hopeless. There is no need for dejection and retreat. The certitude of the theory gives strength to carry on with the relentless search for hidden goods, even when the first few shops turn you away. Once your hearing is refined enough to understand that the reply: 'We haven't got it', really means 'It's under the counter', you will never be overwhelmed by hopelessness. Getting 'No' for an answer simply means: in this particular shop, the assistant either couldn't or didn't want to play the game.

The customer goes from shop to shop, by car, so no unseemly queues are formed. Helpful parking regulations prevent waiting for a chance delivery. Our society has no need for loiterers; those queueing in the bad old days were wasting precious time, instead of building socialism. Furthermore, they were constantly spreading wicked rumours about shortages.

Today, no decent person would stoop to spreading rumours. They spread the good news about hidden sources instead. In the proud knowledge of their civic responsibilities, they don't waste time loitering around the shops; they drive from one shop to the next, conscious of their dignity as human beings, and bribe the sales people. Their refined sense of hearing tells them that 'there is no such thing as a thing that doesn't exist'. This may be called the 'law of non-existence'. It means that the thing really and truly doesn't exist *in that particular place*. It won't arrive now or ever. In that case you have to go in search of it. This law guided us at the time when we booked the fitters for electricity, water, central heating… without having had pipes, radiators and the like. Had we put our trust in the Customer Advisory Service of the Houseware Trust, we would still be nowhere nearer to piping than the immovable samples in their showrooms.

In recent years, quite a few manufacturing or wholesaling outfits have opened customer advisory bureaux. They are friendly, comfortable places, like the one demonstrating oil burners. They are especially inviting in winter, when it's cold in the car going from shop to shop; you can alway drop in at a customers' bureau to thaw out. They are quite successful copies of western civilisation: deep armchairs, potted palms, courteous behaviour. The computers, which ought to control stock levels throughout the trade network, haven't arrived yet. All that our customer service bureaux tell us at the moment is hardly more informative than the notorious posters of olden days, which said: 'If you want a pair of shoes, go to a shoe-shop.' Sometimes their information is even less precise.

I was looking for ready to assemble cupboard units. At the building centre, they very kindly told me that there was only one store dealing in cupboards. They had no idea whether that store had any but obligingly phoned it — the store had none. Sorry, they said, there's far too much building going on, that causes the shortage. A few days later, looking for window glass, I stopped at another store, full of cupboards.

These service bureaux may be no good as far as the quality, availability or whereabouts of various goods are concerned, but they still have their uses. Other customers, would-be builders, also drop in there and they are usually an unfailing source of information as to what's around, where, and how much. This is, therefore, the true vocation of these bureaux. The tips of peripatetic customers are better than the data coming out of the most advanced computer. They can tell you not only about the goods but also about those selling them. You can leave the bureau fully briefed.

The pretty pattern of the wallpaper at the service bureau is never disfigured by sales literature. All they display is tasteful photos of their products. They don't confuse prospective buyers with extraneous information. Least of all would they direct them to a competitor. They are firm upholders of their own trademark. I don't think a service bureau has ever sent a customer to a co-op, or a co-op to a wholesaler — let alone to the private sector. This company chauvinism has its advantages: a less determined group of customers would give up the search and hand over the whole job of procurement to a private sector merchant or artisan. This contractor buys, of course, in bulk from the state concern or the co-op, at wholesale prices and will include in the prices the hassle and bother of chasing after supplies. Usually they will have regular channels to the appropriate sales assistants, who, therefore, can recoup on this particular round-about what they may have lost by sulky and impatient customers not paying 'thanksgiving money'. The recalcitrant customer will thus pay the bribe anyway, through the contractor's invoice, in which the slush money is included.

It's all very different in the private sector. Go to a private motor mechanic's workshop and you'll see the walls covered with relevant advertisements: bodywork, diagnostics, tyre repairs, exhaust fitting, whatever you like. These honest artisans aren't jealous either, they help you with their contacts. A cabinetmaker I know helped me find radiator enamel, which is really scarce, through established channels used mostly for thinners. Cabinetmakers use thinners by the gallon; my friend was in the habit of paying a regular retainer to the manager of a wholesaling firm, so had no trouble getting the thinner in ten-gallon drums, instead of the pricey one-pint bottles. He took me to the source and, while his drum was being lowered by the goods lift to the basement, he mentioned to the manager in passing that a little radiator enamel wouldn't come amiss. Lo and behold, when the lift came up again, there was my radiator enamel. The faces of other would-be buyers were interesting to behold when they spotted the coveted label.

The customer service departments offer a glaring contrast to this friendly give-and-take, with their one-dimensional thinking, their company chauvinism, their jealousy of competitive trade-marks. According to a newspaper, 2 billion forints a year are spent on advertising — to what end, I wonder? Go to the building centre, you'll see a single brick in their shopwindow. Sometimes they create a tasteful symmetry by pairing it with a mosaic tile, or, less appositely, with an aspidistra. Thus, the shopwindow has generally lost its original function of display. Nobody takes it as a signal of availability.

This attitude has its effect on production too. Directors can short-change sales assistants not only by ordering too much or too little — they may also fail to ensure optimal profitability. An excellent example of this is Perlite — an ingenious Hungarian invention. It's a near-perfect heat-and-sound insulating material, made of quarry rubble. This is heated to 2,000 degrees centigrade; the heat turns the stone molecules into bubbles. These are cooled and the bubbles petrify. All you need is stone rubble and heat. Production costs are minimal. In spite of this, Perlite is always scarce. The secret lies in transport: stone remains stone and, while a bag of Perlite costs 20 forints, one waggonload only represents 5,000 forints' worth. Hiring a waggon costs more than the whole profit margin. Perlite is hardly ever advertised, there is very little going for export; demand, nevertheless, is always very strong. The result is that when a supply of Perlite happens to arrive at the building centre, the employees get hold of their rightful share of profits through 'thanksgiving money' rather than the bonus that ought to have been paid to them had the director made a greater effort to increase company profits.

Another variant of this syndrome is a case shown on TV: another useful Hungarian invention, this time a new type of textured plaster with a life expectancy of 40 years, instead of the usual four for conventional stuff. The price is half of that of the old material, including transport costs. Companies are, however, chary of buying it, in spite of fairly heavy advertising by the inventive mining company: by using this cheaper and more durable plaster, they would have to reduce their purchasing budget, the main source of earnings for company and employees alike.

We ourselves had to suffer from this institutional exclusiveness throughout our chase for water pipes. Earlier on, while chasing galvanised sheets for the plumber, we had stumbled on a co-op store — a veritable Aladdin's cave. The kitchenware services bureau had not deigned to mention its existence. We got all the sheets we wanted; now they gave us a good two-thirds of piping needed without demanding a single penny in 'thanksgiving money'. The trouble was that we had to search high and low for the rest, buying in four separate places, including one at a store near Lake Balaton, of all places. And we had to go through the full gamut of approaches described by the oft-quoted clothing director.

Our experience showed very clearly the deplorable lack of co-operation among various sales organisations. Had the attitude of kitchenware services employees not been shaped by company chauvinism but a broader network of mutual interests, both they and the co-op would have profited from such a bargain. The co-op could welcome all the frustrated buyers shunted to it by kitchenware, the co-op shelves would soon be laid bare and co-op sales personnel could add to their meagre salary by pushing popular items under the counter. Kitchenware employees would gain too: once the bounty at the co-op were consumed by the customers directed there, some of them would have to come back to kitchenware stores willy-nilly, and the amount of bribery would inevitably increase.

Admittedly it would be difficult to overcome the structural differences between the two types of organisation. Goods ordered from the factory arrive through different channels.

The advantage to the turnover of the co-op — and corresponding disadvantage to the pocket of the co-op sales assistant — is a result of the greater flexibility of this smaller outfit, as well as of the ingrained habits of many customers, enthralled by the prestige of the bigger organisation. Kitchenware stores get their supplies through a centralised purchasing office in direct contact with the factory; their own procurement officers only deal with internal requirements. At the co-op, the two functions are carried out by one and the same person. They are their own chaser: if there is something out of stock, they can go round in a pick-up van and restock within days. At the kitchenware trust, there is an annual procurement plan; the factory delivers the goods, according to plan, to the central warehouse of the trust; its retail stores place their orders with the warehouse. If, say, a type of piping becomes scarce, the replacement order goes first to the warehouse; the stock controller there notifies central purchasing; thence, the order goes to the factory. Provided the factory has some surplus over and above its export contingent, the whole slow and stately gavotte will be repeated in the opposite direction.

This inertia is, of course, an irritation to expectant customers. Some of them try to short-circuit the lengthy process of procurement and by use of the network (in a state concern, an extensive bureaucracy sits on top of the business organisation) will attempt to divert a consignment en route. Others will stream across to the co-op, on a hit-and-miss basis: it's more difficult to find out where and how its managers are enmeshed in the mutual network. A third group, bedazzled by the citywide advertisements of the kitchenware trust, (or, perhaps, with more intimate links to a particular sales assistant) will settle down and wait for the goods to arrive. These misguided people then pay 'thanksgiving' to the kitchenware sales assistant in consideration of the time and trouble taken getting hold of the precious piping.

Kitchenware sales assistants could earn much more. They ought to recognise they are in the worst position, in terms of supply. On the face of it, in the building industry the state trusts have priority on supplies from state factories, the co-ops get less, the private sector even less. However, the lack of flexibility in a large organisation is the cross sales assistants have to bear; the more flexible co-op and, in particular, the most flexible private sector operator is able to match demand with supply more easily than the state Behemoth. The private sector may cost more, but prices at the co-op are the same as at the trust's retail stores.

Kitchenware sales assistants get the worst deal. In theory, they have the broadest range of goods but get the least 'thanksgiving money'. It would be more sensible for them to send clients over to the co-op as soon as shortages arise; however flexible it may be, the co-op couldn't stand up to the rush, its purchasing officers would be overwhelmed, the factory couldn't supply them with suddenly increased orders. By and by, co-op deliveries would slow down too, the abundance of goods would disappear, to the greater good of all those concerned in the trade. The field would be open for building up the same community of interests as reigns amongst 'black' lorry drivers.

I developed a natural aversion towards the big organisations, in view of their lack of professional solidarity. The sophisticated environment did not satisfy me when genuine customer service was absent. I returned to the stores near large-scale building sites which are always full of all sorts of things. The reception may be in a derelict shed, without deep armchairs and patterned wallpaper, but customer service is open and straightforward. There is no 'thanksgiving', only 'money'. I bought my cupboards there. The dictum of the helpful young lady at the building centre is actually reversed here. There's lots of building going on, but more than enough cupboards. The manufacturer knows the nature of its labour force and knows the rate of breakages. Besides, the prefabricated elements may come out all crooked; difficult — if not impossible — to squeeze into the allotted space. So the storekeeper is allowed a percentage of breakages; he may also persuade — not with fine words alone

— the delivery men not to smash the units to smithereens; he can also accept his fair share of ill-fitting units. This way he can sell fitted cupboards for half the price. Did you want doors or windows too? It's a fact that these stores carry stocks that are perpetually in short supply in the shops. For instance, the only missing piece of piping, a chromium-plated elbow, turned up at one such store, after its very existence had been denied at the centre. Alternatively, the building workers may be as generous with pipes and things, as they are with clamps, copper wire or beams.

I have never approved of theft. The risks are greater than the likely outcome. I've never understood some of my neighbours who made a sport of stealing. One night they swiped a manhole-cover from the street — it was so heavy they could hardly lift it into the car. Another time they 'borrowed' a huge reinforced concrete beam from a site, with the help of a 'black' lorry driver. This was silly, in my opinion: after lighting up time, most people go home to watch the telly, the roads are empty, except for police cars. If the cops catch you, they go through your whole house with a fine-toothed comb. Is it worth a prison sentence?

I didn't object so much to a neighbour who collected a full set of scaffolding from abandoned building sites. Whenever a building firm moves away, or when the electricity board replaces lamp-posts with concrete columns, loads of timber are left to rot. It's hard not to yield to temptation.

While I disagree with thievery, I must admit it represents a higher stage of social development. In earlier times, hooligans vandalised telephone booths, tore the directories to pieces, ripped out the cable, smashed the coinbox for the money. Now they carefully lift the plate-glass windows of the telephone boxes and — commendably perhaps — build it into the dividing door between kitchen and dining room. The glass door of the telephone booth becomes part of the well-appointed, attractive home, instead of mouldering in a dirty underpass. They take away the brass brackets, bolts and nuts too. People sensitive to the beautification of their homes cease to be vandals. With the increase in number of private houses, street vandalism decreases.

There was one particular shop that offered all the advantages of customer service — official and unofficial. The sales personnel did not ask for money, indeed, they were grateful for your friendly behaviour. This was a carpet shop, and soon enough I became a regular caller — if for no other reason, for a friendly chat with the assistants there. My TV-friend called my attention to the place — he discovered it in the course of an outside broadcast and was quite taken by the enthusiasm of the assistants for acting as extras; for them, it was an exciting way to earn a little pin money in employer's time, at their place of work. My reception was equally friendly, even though I did not disclose that I was a friend of the producer.

Their shop was hardly bigger than a boutique, in the centre of the shopping district. Previously I had gone the rounds of carpet specialists, the furnishing departments of large stores, I even visited the international trade fair, in the hope that I might come across some fine carpet of western origin. Alas, ministries and other public bodies unfairly earmarked for themselves the most attractive exhibits. These carried the 'Sold' label even before the opening of the fair.

The splendid Western products only whetted my appetite. Home-made carpet, used in new housing, cost 126 forints per square yard — and is rather poor quality. A better grade cost around 400 forints and one, almost acceptable, around 500. We needed 75 square yards — near 35,000 forints at best, way beyond our budget.

The carpets at the friendly boutique were of a Danish make. I was particularly taken by a wine-coloured, high-pile sample. I could have taken it away, it was so light, no more than a few ounces, and this was the snag. There was so little of it. The Danish factory delivered only its remnants to the Hungarian outlet. The assistants assured me that now and again they received longer lengths, only there wasn't any telling when. Apparently, whenever a containerful of remnants piles up at the Copenhagen factory, they dump it on the boutique in Budapest. The selling price is 25 forints per square yard, less than half the price of the cheapest Hungarian product. God only knows who set up the deal. Maybe it's a foretaste of the next five-year house-building plan, in which room sizes will be adapted to the sizes of carpet offcuts.

"Just stick it out," the assistants said. One day — wonder of wonders — I spotted a Danish container lorry not far from the shop. I rushed over, arriving before the driver and unloading crew.

I asked the assistants if I could help with unloading and slipped in among the others. The carpet rolls were anything but lightweight this time. It was, the assistants said, an exceptional delivery, with so many complete lengths in it. My favourite pattern came in several colours, and I was able to devote myself to the serious business of sorting and selecting to my heart's desire. Again, I got what I wanted for one tenth of the price, at 4,000 forints. A perfect example of the correct purchasing procedure, halfway between miracle and luck: in this deal, there was no need for string-pulling or palm-greasing.

Which goes to show that knowing how to handle people can be as valuable as money. That's why our kind of society can claim to be superior to other systems based on the cash nexus. Human endowments are supreme: just as you cannot buy the quality of the moonlighter's craft by mere money, you have to develop special skills in order to perform quality control over the goods supplied by state commerce. A guarantee card, for instance, is just a piece of paper; it has, perhaps, some validity in systems where bureaucracy does not work for its own advantage alone. For goods supplied by state commerce, a warranty must be backed by personal surety. One can't emphasise too strongly the role played by mutual human bonds in purchasing anything.

For instance, I took an immediate fancy to a tasteful three-piece suite in a department store and bought it on the spur of the moment, for 20,000 forints. On delivery, I discovered numerous faults. I called out the store supervisor; he admitted the poor workmanship without quibble. They took it back to the store, now with a price tag reduced by half. Ten days later, I bought the same suite at the sale or return centre, at a quarter of the original price... thanks to the advice of the supervisor, given in exchange for the usual envelope.

Boilers enamelled inside and out are genuinely scarce, there's no point in hunting for them. My mother, through her contacts at the women's council, eventually found the correct link in the network, and the allegedly everlasting boiler arrived at the door. Unfortunately, after two months it sprang a leak. The fitters who came to repair it under guarantee turned up their noses at the fifty forints 'thanksgiving' I offered. The soldering was correspondingly botched. The leakage continued. Next time, I doubled the tip — to no avail. We learned the name of the director of the boiler firm from the embarrassed link-woman at the council. My wife phoned him, as if she were my secretary, announcing me as 'Comrade X'. I took the receiver and gave the director a good dressing down. The director immediately realised I was in the network and gave me the ex-directory number of a service establishment, adding the name of the person to be approached. My wife repeated her performance and when I took over, I mentioned the director by name. My intervention now was reinforced twice over: at one level, I used the frightened director, at a higher level, the nameless power I pretended to represent.

Within three days, a brand new replacement boiler was delivered. The fitters persisted in calling me 'comrade' — so much so that my wife too called me 'comrade' for days on end.

We didn't want to move in with our battered old fridge. I wrote to another friend, the one who had supplied the fridge eight years ago; he had no difficulty in contriving the loss of the ten-year guarantee card. It was easier for his firm to despatch to me a brand new three-star fridge, rather than hopelessly dig around in the bureaucratic maze of old paperwork.

We couldn't do the same with our TV set because of the continuing service guarantee. I had inherited the set from my father, complete with guarantee. He didn't actually buy it: the electronics company handed out a few sets to selected comrades 'for observation purposes'. Of course, the observers are also observed — that's why my father had given me the set. He could have taken it to Africa — observation is possible there too — the only snag being that TV engineers are not given passports to go out and service sets ailing abroad. At irregular intervals, engineers came along to observe whether we were faithfully observing, which we were.

This, to my mind, was the most highly developed example of the mutual network. The company did not place an obligation on my father for its own selfish interests or for the sake of upstaging the competition. The TV-set was more a token of the whole system built on mutual favours and obligations. Those receiving the token cannot reciprocate directly. Most of them, like my father, had nothing to do with the electronics firm. The act of presentation simply reinforces the habit of mutual favours among the elect and select of the land. The company rendered an inestimable service, by this generous act, to the whole national economy. This benevolent attitude becomes an ingrained habit. People in influential posts will grant favours as an act of second nature. As a result, obstacles in production are eliminated, commerce is eased, the maze of bureaucracy is unwound — even the ultimate customer will benefit, if and when they are allotted the coveted goods. The TV set becomes a symbol of learning.

It was, therefore, no great surprise to me to find, in a learned sociological journal, that I had been following the main lines of scientific inquiry in which the Propaganda Committee of the Hungarian Socialist Workers' Party was currently engaged. In actual fact, I only wanted to build a house. In the process, I was compelled first to analyse, then to synthesise the ideal approach to acquisition, through the various pathways of the mutual network, the moonlighter syndrome, the necessary scale of bribery and corruption, and their requisite combinations. The Party, following the same lines of enquiry, has come up with a scholarly description of the secondary economy, in a treatise titled 'The Structure of Class and Social Strata in Present-Day Hungarian Society'. A pity that, while engaged in chasing the wherewithal for uninterrupted building, I had no time for reading my favourite journal. But then I was also engaged in putting philosophy into practice.

7. The Work Ends

'And the lights came on in the village.' I must confess, I hadn't fully understood the meaning of this sentence that ended so many stories read at primary school, or later, at secondary school, though it was common both in Hungarian and Russian textbooks. I never felt particularly uplifted by the idea of public utilities being introduced into a tiny village. It was only with my university degree behind me, in the course of my 'postgraduate' studies as described in previous chapters, that I came to understand the impact of utilities on one's innermost feelings.

I suppose they celebrated much like we on our hillside did

the day the sewage engineers arrived. Bedding down the mains sewer was itself important; perhaps even more important was the arrival of machinery from the sewerage authority. The number of garage sites multiplied day by day, thanks to the beneficial effect of the great diggers. Everybody's rubble was cleared in minutes by the huge dumpers. People's capacity for changing their environment speeded up no end. Everyone had the chance to give free rein to their talents as the barriers set up by Nature were broken down. Building operations on the hill took on a new lease of life, now that there were so many willing moonlighters at hand. One could hardly move in the narrow streets from the heavy lorries. The people of the plains and hill folk met in a joyous reunion, new friendships abounded; there was no more need to go hunting for 'black' haulage at the other end of the city: they stopped at your doorstep, unloading all kinds of things. It is said that in Britain milk is left at your door every day. Once we complete the edifice of pure communism, no doubt we shall enjoy the same service with sand, gravel and the like.

With the arrival of the sewer-laying teams, our whole situation changed in a dramatic manner. One helpful team after another passed by, checking half-built houses to see what missing item they could offer. Complete gangs came along, offering to lay concrete or fit windows, for 30-40 forints per hour; single hawkers knocked on doors, offering tools, components, even machines.

I had no idea at the time where to turn for the hire of heavy machinery. Without the appearance of the cheerful sewage workers, I wonder, whose crane would have lifted the heavy concrete roof on to the top of my garage? How would I have sunk the oil tanks in their pits? Who would have removed the tons of rubble? I just had to pass on the word and along came the excavator (in employer's time). The operation was very economical on fuel, too, as it only had to travel up the road. Other members of the highly efficient team came along with their dumper lorries and removed rubble and earth in a few turnabouts. The whole deal cost me no more than 2,400 forints.

And so I became an integral part of the sewage company's yearly plan; besides, my part of the plan was carried out with greater enthusiasm than the official one. After all, I did not hinder the work with administrative measures, I didn't try to slow it down or speed it up with tedious attempts to square up this job with others in the plan. The arbitrary division between employer's time and one's own time disappeared — everyone worked here according to mood or needs. As far as the company's employees were concerned, this enterprise was better than a collective holiday. It is doubtful that the workers could have enjoyed the healthy mountain air and, at the same time, have found such satisfying extra work elsewhere. As a bonus, they were allowed to bring their own tools and machines on holiday. This particular team had previously worked almost exclusively on inner city jobs, with hardly any pickings; all they could lay their hands on were a few miserly plumbing repair jobs, where these hadn't already gone to more alert moonlighters. On our hill, there was no such competition. The whole hillside was full of admiration for the sewage workers and their company — and the workers themselves seemed happy too.

The arrival of this crew was a signal in itself. But that was not enough, they needed an organiser. It was B who arranged the extra jobs, working like a beaver. When we first met, in the early days of pipe-laying, he was scheduling jobs for a host of customers. He organised a courier service, to signal the arrival of the works supervisor, explained to him that so-and-so had just nipped off to buy cigarettes, sent someone to bring back team members from private jobs. He allotted the machinery for the different tasks too; all in all, he succeeded in creating perfect balance between official sewage work and private engagements. His organising talent was bolstered by a strong social conscience. He took great care to ensure there would be no injustice in sharing paid overtime; at the same time, he was meticulous in making sure that no team-mate should clock up a suspiciously high number of overtime hours, when he was actually doing some private job. B was as good as the best trade-union officer.

He arranged the grab and the dumpers for my house, but that was only the beginning. Seeing the botched job F and his mate — the pseudo-bricklayers — had done, B organised a team of proper bricklayers for us. He recruited a specialist for the insulation work. He had contacts beyond the sewerage brigade too. He blossomed forth, practically before my eyes, into a semi-independent building contractor. From the top of the hill he surveyed the land below him: in many places the work-force owed allegiance to him. But he cast his eyes further than the city spreading below us, as far as his home village: in the case of urgent need, he was able to recruit labourers from the village inn.

He brought from his village a couple of gypsies to do the insulation work. There is no cheaper labour and none more careful. B arranged the insulation for my neighbours too; we were all full of praise for the quality of work. The gypsies adored him, their benefactor — in the villages, the number of jobs insulating concrete foundations has always been less than the gypsy birthrate. Wherever B arrives with the pipe-laying team, his faithful followers come after; his social conscience always makes sure gypsies are paid above average village earnings.

B called on his customers in a very conscientious manner, once a day, to check on progress. We were on good terms soon enough: sometimes he borrowed money off me, repaying it meticulously the following day. When I asked him about a plasterer, he just jotted down a name and telephone number on the edge of a newspaper for me and drove off, without indicating the expected fee. When I phoned the plasterer, he was rather abrupt in his refusal and only became more forthcoming when I mentioned B's name. He was booked months ahead, he said, both at home in his village and in the city.

What did he charge a square yard? I asked the now friendlier voice (F and his mate, before their ignominious departure, had charged 40 forints for plain walls and 45 forints for ceilings). 30 forints, said the voice on the line. Well, couldn't he rearrange the bookings, if I paid 35 forints? He would have to talk it over with his partner, he said, he'd let me know tomorrow.

Next day, the partner turned up sooner than the plasterer himself. Their booking system wasn't so strict after all. He had been helping a neighbour build a house and could leave it, he said. Actually, the reason he was so prompt was he wanted to sell his cement-mixer. He was shrewd enough to suspect that its price would be higher in the city. He was right: I bought the machine for 6,000 forints. B, in generous gesture, delivered the mixer to me free of charge. At the end of our job, I passed it on to my neighbour for 7,000.

Cement-mixers have since ceased to be in short supply. You

can now buy them off the shelf for 10,000 forints. A much sought-after article would be withdrawn from distribution for a while, then put back on the market with slight modifications, at a higher price. The private sector adapted itself to this process in a flexible manner. For instance, there'd be a small ad in the papers, offering home-made cement mixers at 14,000 forints each. The man who assembled them would be booked up for a couple of months ahead; knocking them together in two days at most and making a killing in the market. When mixers reappeared in the shops, he would simply switch to another piece of equipment that happened to be in short supply.

There are a number of machines only needed occasionally; there is no generalised demand for them, worth the time and effort of the small engineering workshop. Take the Swiss 'Hilti' concrete drill, easily available, with a complete set of drill-heads, at any merchant in town, for 80,000 forints. It's only needed for drilling holes into concrete. If this is what you need to do, there's a specialist with his drill available to do it. He charges 150 forints an hour to recoup his investment. Our way to this specialist was less direct. The assembled crowd of electricians, heating engineers and plumbers were one day amazed to see us lying prostrate on the concrete floor, with hammers and chisels. The trouble was that we could not find the drainage hole for the water conduit from the house — the previous builder either didn't cater for it or didn't bother to tell us where to look for it. In a couple of hours, we succeeded in gouging a hole exactly one eighth of an inch deep, — on which basis we would need over 500 hours to get through the thickness of the concrete.

The merciful artisans couldn't bear to see our predicament and, after enjoying the spectacle for a while, gently informed us about the concrete drilling specialists. Their grapevine worked faster than any small ad and along came Mr C. He was a friend of a friend of a plumber. His pick-up van groaned under the weight of the big Hilti drilling machine.

Mr C was a chartered accountant in daytime; in the evenings and weekends, he rolled up his shirtsleeves, loaded his Hilti and started on his drilling rounds. It had all started with his dog. He had a large retriever, with whom he'd lived peacefully in his bachelor flat, on one of the wooded hills surrounding the city. Then one fine day, his landlord sold the house, flat included, and Mr C and the hound were shunted to a one-room flat on a new housing estate. Gone were the days when the dog could roam around on the hillside; the playground at the edge of the estate was hardly large enough to exercise a chihuahua. Mr C, having been an honest accountant all his life, could not hope to save up enough for a house in the hilly districts, and there was very little call for his learned services outside his job.

Walking his dog sadly in the dusty enclosure, he soon noticed the mad rush after a man with a drill, and followed the progress of this man from flat to flat with increasing interest. Being an essentially modest man, at first he bought an electric nail-punch and started on his rounds offering his services. 10 forints per nail was his fee, the same as the going rate. However, soon enough all the shelves, picture-rails and kitchen cabinets were in place on the estate; once the great wave of new tenants ebbed away, demand for his nail-punch subsided.

He came to the conclusion that, as the rate of communal house-building was diminishing, the number of privately built houses must increase, given that the number of would-be house-owners was growing all the time. New houses use a lot of concrete; and concrete often needs drilling. Besides, his dog would have a free run on private plots.

His modest profits from the nail-punch were not enough for a desirable residence, but just about covered the investment of the Hilti drill. Today, Mr C is living in a suburban villa, with a large garden; in the day his dog can bark at other dogs from behind the rails — in the evenings, he can bark at the dogs of prospective house-owners, while his master drills into the concrete. Mr C is making 8,000 forints clear profit every month from his Hilti drill. He has only one competitor, a man with a proper trade licence, whose small ads regularly appear in the papers; according to Mr C, this man is also inundated with jobs, but on top of these he has to deal with time-consuming tax affairs, being a licensed trader. The drill has done a lot of good to Mr C in other ways too: his arm muscles are as thick as those of a weightlifter. It took him six hours to drill through our 20-inch concrete foundation. He charged 800 forints for the job and, like the good book-keeper he was, he carefully entered the job in his little notebook. The work well and truly done, drill and dog went back into his van, he rolled down his sleeves, carefully knotted his tie, put on his well-cut jacket (of pure English cloth) and became again the perfect gentleman.

Once we had a drain, there were no further obstacles to the installation of the water system. It took two weeks for the plumber to complete this, with the help of two eager mates: my partner and myself. Actually, the plumber was employed by my partner's company; that accounted for his very reasonable charge, 11,000 forints for the two flats. All the tools came from his place of work, we supplied the materials. His price included a further visit later on, to fit the units once plastering and decorating were finished. In the course of the work, we became expert plumbers ourselves: the master did not begrudge us his knowledge, particularly as he owed allegiance to my partner. (Nor did he want constant recriminations from a colleague, had something gone wrong.) He was the kind of artisan who likes to give a running commentary. It was a perfect audio-visual training course. Plumbing is a somewhat simpler craft than plastering or tile-laying, where many years' experience is needed to get the hang of various tricks of the trade. Having learnt my lesson from the sad story of the guttering, I was quite keen to store up some plumbing knowledge for the future.

These weeks spent on linking up the utilities was a polytechnic education, in the literal sense of the word. The curriculum covered plumbing, electrical engineering, plastering and cental heating. Getting a good heating engineer was slightly more complicated than enticing the plumber. In my uncle's block of flats, the boilers were maintained by an old fitter, employed by the district housing authority. I asked for his advice — that was all he could give, as he was too old to undertake the whole job in our house himself. He recommended a past apprentice of his, whom I found working as a fitter at the new Hilton hotel. He worked in a foursome, in quite a reputable moonlighting team. Their design engineer was group leader at the Gas Board engineering department.

At my house, the designer immediately suggested a new layout, saving 10,000 forints from the total cost; he only asked 2,500 for the new plan.

The only loser in this business was my partner. His suspicion about me, concerning the concrete radiator substitutes, was so enduring that he refused to have anything to do with the Hilton team. He drew up his own design, based on his cast iron radiators, sharing only the assembly costs.

The Hilton boys did everything with a swagger. Not like the plumber, who expected us to supply all requirements, they brought everything with them from the Hilton Palace hotel, with a royal gesture: pipes, valves, taps, lagging, radiator controls. They were proud to be able to supply us with the most advanced equipment of international industry. Their huge welding machine was worthy of the establishment that had hosted the late lamented Shah of Iran, Jacqueline Kennedy Onassis or the Prince of Wales. The same machinery is in use at the Hilton in Mexico City or the Canary Islands, they said with professional pride. In the space of ten days they finished the job. I would have liked to give them a reception at the Hilton; but staff are not welcome in the cocktail bar.

Electricity was more difficult. A letter of guarantee is essential, as the Electricity Board will not connect the house up to the mains without it. Guarantee letters can only be issued by state concerns, co-ops or licensed private sector engineers. We had nothing against the state firms or the co-op (indeed, many of our contributors came from them) but our faithful moonlighters were not entitled to issue the document, let alone attach to it the great big stamp required. So, for the first time in the operation, we had to get in touch with the private sector.

We didn't have to look through the yellow pages to find the right person: my wife knew someone, though in a somewhat roundabout way. It all went back to her youthful enthusiasm for a particular pop group.

Our engineer had inherited his licence from his father, an honest, old-fashioned electrician. The father's only ambition was to secure his son's future, by teaching him a skill and leaving him a going concern. However, the son didn't care much for electricity: his obsession was music. The father was strong-willed enough to compel his son to take part in a regular training course; the son, however, turned his newly acquired skills to his own Bohemian purposes. His popularity in the pop-music world was as much due to his wizardry with the electronics of various pop groups, as to his guitar. Soon enough, he worked with the best beat bands.

While his father was alive, he led a double life: he left home in the morning, a poor but honest electrician and returned late at night, a pop star. He handed over all his earnings to his father; the old man observed with apparent satisfaction the results of his principles. The boy kept quiet about the source of his artistic earnings; it was all due to overtime, or the result of socialist competition, he said.

The father tried to match his son's income by taking on more and more private jobs, with tragic consequences: he died from overwork. On his deathbed his last words were about his hope that his son's tremendous devotion to his job would restore the honour of honest private craftsmanship.

When my wife revived the memory of the times when she had been a fan of the electric guitarist, he was touched by her devotion and willingly undertook the wiring of our house. For friendship's sake, he only charged 10,000 forints, including the official guarantee. Components, cables and other supplies came from the demolished factory, first-class West German material. His mate was an old employee of his father's who — with another touching adherence to tradition — didn't ask for more than 15 forints per hour. He mostly arrived half drunk. My partner made up for the failings of the old man, taking a lion's share of the wiring.

The 10,000 forints thus largely paid for the signature of the artist. Of course, P, my partner and myself could have done the whole job ourselves, but with no hope of Board approval. However, when I reported completion and asked for connection, referring to the number of our friend's license, the Electricity Board inspectors promptly arrived.

On the appointed day they turned up in their car, strolled round the house poker faced, occasionally stopping to contemplate the finer points of the building. The music-loving electrician had warned us that the inspection would cost money (he must have learnt that much from his father) but had no idea about the rate for the bribe, nor did he know the inspectors personally. I had to play it by ear.

I invited them in; the doorbell didn't work yet, that depended on the outcome. They entered, ambled round and dropped extremely derogatory remarks about the work. One of them belittled the external wiring, especially the meter-reading box; the other one disparaged the bathroom switch and the boilerhouse controls. I followed them silently, while they made their way round the house. In the end, they became quite emotional in their joint condemnation.

I kept quiet throughout, and when they were about to leave, politely asked them to tell me what needed doing. They listed 16 items, with a total cost appreciably higher than the whole wiring. After reading through the list, I turned to the inspectors saying:

"Let's talk seriously," and put down two 100-forints notes. "Now, what's to be repaired?"

They pocketed the notes, and one of them said:

"Bend this hook with a plier." The other one said:

"Give the box a lick of paint."

Two days later, the electricity board van stopped in front of the house, the engineers connected us up to the mains — and the lights came on in the house.

Next came tiling the bathroom. I had already selected my tiles, not because I liked them, but because I disliked them least. They immediately looked prettier, when I was told they'd stopped making them. My new friend P, listening to my tale of woe, dismissed it with a wave of the hand — not directed at me but at the purchasing officer of the co-op. It emerged that the tile factory made a special batch of 600 tiles of that particular pattern, for the daughter of the chairman of the local collective farm. There was some glaze left and it was perfectly possible to make another batch for the co-op buyer, that is for P, that is for me.

P's behaviour was somewhat peculiar these days. He suspected a rival in the person of B. Although his fears were groundless, he tried his hardest to outdo the object of his jealousy. Over and above his constant flow of material supplies, he also started hiring labour — (B couldn't care less about such emotions, he was too busy with organisation) — for instance, tile-layers, who did the job for 35 forints, and were able to borrow the co-op's large tile-cutting machine for the weekend.

P overwhelmed me with presents: full bottles of tile adhesive, six boxes of white tiles; smoke-coloured glass tiles for a bathroom mirror.

The white tiles came from two separate hospital operating theatres. One of the outlying hospitals of the city was condemned, then — after a lot of wrangling — reprieved. This type of fine ceramic tile usually costs 6-8 forints each; but at the hospital democracy ruled, professor or porter could buy them (and almost anything else) for next to nothing. Once reprieve was declared, they just wrote off the lot and rebuilt the whole hospital from scratch.

The re-building of the hospital offered a good source of willing tile-layers. A railway waggon stood in the yard, serving as a combined changing-room and store for the workers. While I was waiting for my gang, I spotted some boxes of Italian tiles.

— What is this? — I asked.

— How many do you want? — they said. I backed my car next to the waggon, and they packed it with the lovely Italian stuff, at 2 forints apiece. These pretty beige tiles complement the cream-white ones from the hospital theatre in my bathroom very nicely.

The next thing I got from P was Caminite, an especially hard kind of mortar, used for plastering chimneys and for insulation. P supplied it at 100 forints per hundredweight, instead of the official co-op price of 1,000. In fact, I was doing P a good turn in buying it. He'd overstocked with Caminite, for which demand was much slower than for the ordinary cement. In desperation, he'd tried to flog it to gravestone-masons for use, instead of more expensive artificial stone. I bought enough Caminite from him to lay out the terrace and external stairs.

P's generosity was boundless: next came carpet adhesive, at 1,500 forints instead of the shop price of 4,000. However hard I tried to reciprocate, he always offered me more. He also insisted on helping me lay the carpet.

However, before this, the little matter of the floors had to be settled. Laying the concrete is the hardest job, albeit the cheapest. Friends and neighbours came to pitch in, but we all lacked the skill to make it level. This was a bad time of the year for moonlighting: every company was trying to catch up with the year-end completion of its plan.

My partner's wife was invited at that time to a topping-out ceremony by a colleague. Towards the end of the celebration, she asked the builder what his next job was. The man told her that he was leader of a builder's gang at a co-op in the outskirts, doing a rush job for the army. They were all under military discipline, with a colonel in charge of operations. The work had such high priority that when it got behind schedule the civilian population was also compelled to do fatigue duty over weekends. Sometimes workers were under virtual house arrest, working from 5 a.m. till retreat.

We smuggled out two bricklayers from under the noses of the guards every evening. The concreting went all right, but we had some trouble with the external plastering. Away from the threatening uniforms, the bricklayers drank too deeply of civilian freedom, not to mention the hard stuff. One of them, standing above me on the scaffolding, accidentally kicked down a cement bucket — it crashed down inches from my head. I didn't fancy becoming a civilian casualty of excessive military discipline.

On the other hand, the workmen did not lose their civility completely: when they saw the kind of paint brushes we had, they pityingly produced far superior ones from their bags and sold them to us at half the going rate. Their brushes must have come from the disbanding of a cavalry regiment: nowadays it's almost impossible to get such fine horsehair-brushes. They were worth their weight in gold, holding the paint marvellously; with our civilian brushes, my whole arm was sopping wet within minutes.

The front of the house had to wait for its finish. I wanted to avoid the usual pebble-dash and dreamt of a snow-white plastic paint — more attractive as well as more durable. The annoying delay was due to the glazier.

This moonlighting glazier turned out to be a rather tricky character. When we approached him, he was working on my partner's mother-in-law's house, on behalf of the borough maintenance department.

My partner met him having lunch with his mother-in-law; the white-haired old artisan, with ruler behind his ear, a reassuring smell of putty around him, made a good impression on my partner. Naturally, he jumped at the chance of glazing our windows. He warned us, it would take time: he would have to save up the glass for us from his allocation for a complete block of flats. We did not mind; we were pretty busy with the utilities. He asked for only a 100 forints per square yard, judged by my partner to be a fair price. Anyway, the old man carried on most of the time castigating our money-grubbing generation. He was more interested in the bygones of the past age. My partner lent an understanding ear, himself having an emotional attachment to the good old days. Once the old man invited him to his house: one could hardly move there from the vast amount of antiques — mostly junk, my partner told us. Cuckoo clocks, guild chests, ikons, horse harness, faîence dishes, railway lamps, branding irons, all jostled one another in a fantastic jumble. The glazier suggested to him there and then that he would willingly forgo the 100 forints, if we could pay him with antiques. My partner promised to go down to the farm and try to lay his hands on a few pitchers, spinning wheels or whatever; it was a somewhat forlorn hope, as the emissaries of the museum had already stripped everything valuable. The glazier was luckily not too finicky about what constituted an antique: everything from the beginning of time till the Russian occupation interested him.

While my partner was scouring the countryside for suitable antiques, the glazier by and by assembled the window-panes from his official allocation; P and I fetched them from his place of work. The glazier did the work over the weekend, and I acted as his mate. I wasn't as enthralled by his work or his running commentary as my partner had been. I thought the window-panes were a little thin for our large picture-windows — wouldn't they collapse under their own weight? The glazier's touching story about the gold old days, when thick glass had been in abundance, sounded a bit suspect. It's all very well to blame the system, but surely not for everything? I felt certain that thicker glass could be had, it only needed going after. Maybe all it required was a somewhat larger bribe. My doubts however weren't strong enough to break the agreement as far as my windows were concerned; the weather was still quite mild, there was no hurry.

The glazier mentioned more than once that he could get hold of Vliesin, the plastic paint I wanted for the frontage. 2,500 forints for a 40-pound can, he said — 8,000 at the shops, — and not always easy to get. One can would do for the whole house-front, as it can be diluted ten to one. We could pay him with antiques, he said, money was of no great interest to him.

This scale of dilution did not sound right, so I went to check up at a chemical retailers. There was plenty of Vliesin there, for only 2,500 forints the 40-pound can — and not to be diluted. Which meant that we needed 160 pounds for the house-front. I went straight over to where the glazier worked and told him outright that he'd get no more than 1,000 a can — for four cans. Within a week, my partner collected the four cans — which proved that money was indeed of no great interest to him. He was sharp enough, though, to beat down the value of the cracked pots my partner collected for him.

My belief in the glazier's truthfulness was somewhat shaken. So I turned to the private sector — principle or no principle. The old man's horror stories proved quite untrue: one private sector glazier quoted 110 forints per square yard, including lovely thick plate glass, way below the 160 the old glazier had tried to frighten me with. This contractor finished the job in a day, and as he came with his own mate, I didn't have to listen to the old man's boring stories either. Although he did try to diddle me, I couldn't really blame him: all he wanted was to ward off the private sector competition, much like the 'black' drivers who stole a march on cheap sand from public sources. Anyway, it was a great day when we climbed up the scaffolding for the last time and applied the plastic paint to our resplendent frontage.

The next problem was the internal staircase. The planks, cut according to the sketches of the carpenter, had duly arrived from Z's timber yard. My cabinetmaker friend came along to assemble it. But when we laid them out, we discovered that some of the treads were incorrectly cut. Was it my mistake, or had Z's minion drunk the whole bottle of wine I'd given him at one go? I did not want to bother Z again for such a trifle, and the cabinetmaker sprang to my help. He had a sculptor friend who occasionally helped him make reproduction furniture, for which special timber was necessary. The sculptor also had a second-string job: he was a forestry engineer. A cushy job by any standards: once a week he climbed up the mountain, for 7,000 forints a month. He could lay his hand on any kind of choice timber; later on, he supplied me with a high quality redwood for my own furniture, the like of which even the oldest cabinetmakers had never seen. This timber was offloaded from a ship in the Danube harbour, specially for him, on company account. Another line of his was smoke-coloured glass. This is mostly used in suave office blocks; he buys up the offcuts and rejects, at 60 forints the square yard (official price: 2,000 forints). What's left from furniture making he sells to private builders at a good margin to himself.

I bought three oaken logs from the sculptor. He'd wanted to carve them, but had no compunction about selling them to me for 1,500 forints, a stiffer price than Z's rate. They were worth it, having matured for years in the yard. P being away, another friend (the one who had supplied the industrial gloves for the brickyard) got hold of a pick-up van from his father's factory at no extra charge, and the trunks were transported to a workshop.

It was at the back of a village-type house, in the old stables. Private sector cabinetmakers didn't keep factory-size wood-working machines in their own workplaces; they came here for large-scale jobs, like planing or turning to low tolerances. Ten large machines stood in the barn, and a number of cabinet-makers, awaiting their turn. The owner of the shop made a liv-ing by hiring his machinery, at 80 forints per hour. By the look of it, he must have inherited the setup from his father, — pro-bably from his grandfather — and kept family traditions in greater honour than the musically-minded electrician: on the machine I used, one could clearly see the date of Napoleon's death. It was worthy of a place in the science museum, but here at least, it earned more than the entrance fee. Counting eight hours' use a day, the 10 machines could have brought in about 150,000 forints a month, even with high taxes and maintenance costs. Certainly, the machine worked without a hitch. For three hours' work, I paid not quite 400 forints. My cabinetmaker friend had warned me not to argue about the actual time I'd used. It was the privilege of the owner to charge more or less, according to his whim. Haggling would have meant a blot in my friend's copybook; besides, I would also need machine time later for my furniture.

As it happened, the owner must have found a kindred spirit in me; he asked me about my business and, when he heard I was furnishing my own house, pricked up his ears. His own house was on the list for expropriation, he said, so he was also looking for a suitable plot. I mentioned the plot above my own, but when he heard that it was only about 50 square yards, he smiled, saying that he'd grown up in the country and wanted at least 150 square yards.

While we were chatting, one of the customers joined us, a

fat, unpleasant-looking character. He wanted to boast about his holiday home, next to the Danube, on top of a hill. It needed a bit of earthwork, a 20-yard high retaining wall — costing not less than 2m forints. At least it's an investment, he said, what else can you spend your money on? With the added advantage that he saw less of his family. The owner didn't like this bragging at all and charged him well over the odds.

The planks properly cut, the staircase was duly erected — it was a great moment to be able to dispense with shaky ladders. Now the plumber was due back, we had to get a bathtub, wash-hand basins, WC bowls. The closing-down sale at the hospital was over. But at least the taps and other accoutrements came free, a gift from a friend of my wife.

This woman was an export buyer. Originally the most promising student in her class at university, she spoke four languages; her essays attracted attention at various international symposia, regardless of the fact that she was not allowed to attend. Bearded scientists forecast a great future in linguistics for her. Regrettably enough, there was no job for her at the university department; the Academy of Sciences cold-shouldered her too, in view of the perennial infighting between the two institutions. For years, she was tossed to and fro, on the waves of empty promises. In the meantime, she did menial jobs at the department, for a ridiculous 1,500 forints' salary squeezed out of the meagre research budget.

One day she had a less scientific but certainly more lucrative offer from a smallish export-import outfit. The task of this unit was to establish links between Hungarian firms not having the right to direct foreign trading, and their overseas partners. So she could satisfy her heart's desire (denied her in her student days) to visit the medieval towns in countries whose languages she had learnt with such devotion.

She was being paid 6,000 forints by the agency to represent the overseas customer. It so happened that one of these was a manufacturer of bathroom furniture — taps, valves and the like. Her task was to arrange compensation deals: foreign equipment in exchange for Hungarian goods, not currency. It is in the interest of foreign exporters — struggling in their own saturated markets — to open up promising new areas. Around Christmas, their gifts land regularly under her tree. One company presented her with four new tyres — worth at least 10,000 forints — another one with a pocket calculator, another with kitchen or bathroom equipment. All samples, of course, or demonstration units, not for sale. Good promotion for the seller.

She, being a good friend, (and having already fitted her own flat with brand new units) presented us with a complete set of bathroom units. Water flows from Austrian taps into Italian basins. The towel-rail, soap-dish and toilet paper-holder are the pride of the West German stainless steel industry. The sample collections of Western firms saved us at least 10,000 forints. I don't think she regrets abandoning linguistics.

One of the last jobs was enamelling the radiators. We had the enamel, but we had no spray-gun. After a short but fruitless search among friends and acquaintances, our next-door-but-one neighbour came to the rescue. He was a lecturer at a nearby technical college. The full range of machinery at the college was put at our disposal, including a spray-gun. As it turned out, my postgraduate studies had been far from complete.

We agreed with this new neighbour that the third thesis set up by Marx in his critique of Feuerbach's philosophy was still valid: 'The materialist doctrine concerning the changing of circumstances and education forgets that circumstances are changed by people and that the educators must themselves first be educated.' I introduced the lecturer to P's trade network, linked him up with B's flying labour squad and secured some timber for him through Z. I was glad to be able to pass on my accumulated wisdom and experience. In exchange, I had the free run of the most modern machinery available at the college, enabling me to reduce quite considerably the time required by various moonlighters, as well as making it unnecessary to resort to the machine shop in the outskirts. Over and above this, I was invited to make suggestions about the improvement of the college machine park, within the framework of its official budget. Being an attentive teacher, the neighbour asked me in minute detail about the tasks that might yet emerge in the course of our operations, and what sort of new machinery might be required.

One of the tasks still ahead of me was polishing the artificial stone terrace. The lecturer persuaded his director, without any great difficulty, that his workshop could not really carry on any longer without an electric stone-polisher; this was purchased straightaway and put at my disposal. When one of the oil tanks sprang a leak, we brought the aluminium-welding maching up from the college. The huge thing weighed at least half a ton. This gave me a good opportunity to lecture the lecturer on methods of hiring black lorries. We stopped one before the college gate, and the welder was driven up the hill for 50 forints.

The lecturer, naturally, did not buy his plot of land from his modest salary. His source of income is from building machines in his workshop, from college materials and with college tools. He teaches his students how to assemble the machines — how to sell them is the subject of a separate business studies course. What happens to the assembled units once the class is over is, of course, nobody's business. The lecturer's main line was woodworking machinery. Every week he assembled a circular saw — this needs so little in the way of materials that nobody notices — and sold it to one of his regular cabinetmaker customers.

His technique resembles that of a collective farm manager, who only needs to observe the permitted percentage of breakages marked on the advice note delivering eggs — the number that did not actually break is his profit. Just for friendship's sake, the neighbour rigged up a small electric saw for me from a spare electric motor and a few odds and ends. It came in very useful making furniture.

This neighbour, teacher and friend is the most helpful and generous person I know. Every morning, as he goes to work, he calls in to ask whether I need anything. If so, I am free to come down to the college after hours (he has his own key to the workshop). Smaller items — drills, hand tools and the like — he simply brings along. These are all disposables. After all, the students are breaking things all the time, there's a constant stream of replacement items. He fetches hacksaw blades by the dozen; true, they only cost 4 forints apiece, but sawing water pipes uses up an awful lot. It was his rule that there had to be at least 300 hacksaw blades in his workshop stock, and no questions asked. And who would count the constant stream of bolts, nuts and screws?

The sewage workers finished their job, all utilities were now linked up. One job remained: laying the tarmac on the drive to the garage, both at my house and at the lecturer's. We worked as a well-practised team. The lecturer went down to the college, to carry on welding the balustrade for my terrace. I kept a lookout for the road-menders. The smoke from the tar-boiler was visible throughout the morning, two streets lower down; but it did not move. I strolled down and found the workers dozing on the lukewarm tarmac. Hearing the good news about some private business, they were on their feet in a second, the tar-laying machine puffed up the hill, followed by the steam-roller and a lorry with paving stones.

Everything was now complete in and around the house. And so was my education. I had fully graduated at the university of life.

Epilogue

The tarmac people finished. The house suddenly stood still. But the momentum of feverish activities pursued over the last few months still excited me. What would I do next? Translation for 25 forints per hour — 50, if I'm lucky — and die of boredom? All right, I'd finish the translation suspended during house-building, but then I'll stop. I only did translations in the hope that something better might turn up; now it had. Through the window, I could see the departing smoke of the tar-layer. I can see through my walls the line of water-pipes, the conduits for electric cables, the linkages of radiators with the boiler and further on, the oil tank; I can see through the Hungarocell insulation. If I am prepared to keep P sweet, drop in occasionally at Z's office, the house will not enclose me or freeze me into immobility. Why should I shut off this new world, a source both of amusement and of profit?

It would be wrong to let all that activity, still pulsating in the walls, seep away, to let the house become just an object. That would be alienation.

I could sell it for a million and a half to the first comer, I'm sure. Then I could buy the next plot and start all over again. Now I know I could build it for less than the 560,000 forints it actually cost, I could have another year's entertainment. Repetition, though, would reduce the pleasure. I would only postpone the real question: how could I make a living from my knowledge?

I could keep the house and, using my recently acquired wisdom, become a full-time building contractor. Above the board or under the counter, what did it matter? My colleagues of old would be surprised — so what? Their concerns don't interest me any longer. This way I would benefit both myself and the community — but wouldn't I get bored by routine tasks? To be a bored millionaire is just as bad as being a bored pauper.

As a building contractor, I could coin money. That's just the trouble: how to spend it? Of course, I could always invest it in other ventures. Respecting my father's wishes, I would not invest it in the syndicate. Anyway, the syndicate is still teetering on the borderline of legality. On the other hand it would be impossible to invest that much money in legal business. I might find myself, sooner or later, in an undesirable place. Translation was easier than hard labour...

That kind of price for the pleasure of contractorship would be too high. Of course, I could find pleasure less spiritual than the rewards of doing good: I could smoke long cigars, or joints — maybe they would offer a vision of a better world. But the intoxication would dull my values and judgement.

What about spending money on earthly goods? But I don't fancy a holiday home, a derelict watermill; another car, with more chromium, doesn't tempt me either. Anyway, goods would just represent more money — another closed circle.

Perhaps, if I could travel to my heart's desire, I might be tempted to turn my undoubted talents to the reduction of the housing shortage. If the powers-that-be would acknowledge the merit of my activities by lifting the barriers at frontier posts, I might even consider becoming an honest taxpayer, a fully licensed building contractor. Alas, this is most unlikely. But who knows? They may take to heart my experiences as related here and recognise the maxim that when you close one door, another will invariably open.